THAT ALL MAY GO WELL

Why Christians Prosper, Why They Don't, and Why It Doesn't Matter

COY D. ROPER

CYPRESS
PUBLICATIONS

That All May Go Well: Why Christians Prosper, Why They Don't, and Why It Doesn't Matter
Published by Cypress Publications

Copyright © 2020 by Coy D. Roper

Manufactured in the United States of America

Cataloging-in-Publication Data
Roper, Coy (Coy Dee), 1937–
That All May Go Well: Why Christians Prosper, Why They Don't, and Why It Doesn't Matter/ by Coy D. Roper
p. cm. —
Includes index.
ISBN 978-1-7320483-7-9 (pbk.)
1. Christian stewardship. I. Author. II. Title.
BV772.R66 2020 248.6—dc20
Library of Congress Control Number: 2020900979

Cover design by Brittany McGuire

All rights reserved. No part of this publication may be reproduced, distributed, stored in a retrieval system, or transmitted in any form or by any means without the prior written permission of the publisher, except in the case of brief quotations embodied in critical reviews and certain other noncommercial uses permitted by copyright law.

Select Scripture quotations in this publication are from the Contemporary English Version Copyright © 1991, 1992, 1995 by American Bible Society; the NEW AMERICAN STANDARD BIBLE®, copyright© 1960, 1962, 1963, 1968, 1971, 1972, 1973, 1975, 1977, 1995 by The Lockman Foundation; the Holy Bible, New International Version® NIV® Copyright © 1973 1978 1984 2011 by Biblica, Inc.™; and the New Revised Standard Version Bible, copyright © 1989 National Council of the Churches of Christ in the United States of America. Used by permission. All rights reserved worldwide.

CONTENTS

Preface	v
Introduction: Not the Prosperity Gospel	vii
Part 1 Why Christians Prosper	**3**
1. Because They Work Hard	9
2. Because They Obey the Law	23
3. Because They Practice Christian Virtues	33
4. Because They Act Wisely	45
5. Because They Have Help	55
6. Because They Are Good Stewards	69
Part 2 And Why They Don't	**85**
7. A Matter of Perception	87
8. The Result of Human Weakness	91
9. The Working of God's Will	97
10. Because They Choose Not To	107
Part 3 Why It Doesn't Matter	**113**
11. It Does Matter	115
12. Contentment	119
13. Love of Money	125
14. Different Priorities	133
Conclusion: So What?	143
Scripture Index	149

PREFACE

As a preacher of the gospel and a professor in Christian colleges, I have never been greatly concerned about "prosperity." My parents were school teachers and in later years, missionaries. My brother David is a preacher and a writer, and I don't remember our discussing how we could get rich as we sat around the dinner table when we were kids.

Why then would I write a book on the subject? Primarily because in my fifty-plus years of experience as a preacher and teacher in five states, three countries, and on two continents, I have encountered a number of faithful Christian men and women who had become very prosperous. These were people who were not born into rich families, nor did they appear to be extraordinarily talented. They were just ordinary folks and never pretended to be anything else. Then I noticed that in many congregations most of the members were doing well financially. As I was growing up in Oklahoma, if the subject of money was ever tied to the subject of Christianity, the assumption was that if people were good Christians, they were most likely poor.

So why had these faithful Christians prospered? That led me to thinking. Christians are given a set of instructions. If obeyed, biblical instruction could help a person succeed financially as well as spiritually. So, I decided that this was a subject that needed to be explored—not to convince people that they could get rich if they would become Christians, but to demonstrate to Christians (and to the world) how blessed we are that God has given us a way that leads to happiness in this life, as well as after this life is over. The result of that study was the first section of this book: "Why Christians Prosper."

When I told various family members of my plans to write such a treatise, I heard all kinds of objections. Chiefly these good Christians asked, *"How can you say that Christians prosper when many of them are poor and have so many diverse financial problems?"* That's a fair question and it led to the addition of several caveats to the manuscript and to the creation of a second section of the book about why Christians don't prosper. In addition, I was afraid that writing on this subject might cause someone to think that material prosperity is the most important thing in life, so I added a third section: "Why It Doesn't Matter."

That's how *That All May Go Well* came to be. The title comes from 3 John 2: "Dear friend, I pray that you may enjoy good health and that all may go well with you, even as your soul is getting along well" (NIV). Here's hoping you will learn something from it that will bless your life. And I pray that somehow it will bring glory to God.

Coy Roper
Abilene, Texas

INTRODUCTION

THIS IS NOT THE PROSPERITY GOSPEL

It might be easy for someone to look at the title of this book and conclude: "Oh no, not another book promoting the 'health and wealth gospel.'" (Or to say: "Hallelujah! Another book preaching my favorite Bible doctrine—the 'health and wealth gospel'!")

To make sure that such a thing does not happen, I want here and now to deny that what I am affirming is the "health and wealth gospel." I do not believe that doctrine. In fact, I would affirm that the "prosperity gospel"[1] is a blatant heresy which contradicts plain biblical teachings. To elaborate on that statement, I want to discuss what the health and wealth gospel is and then say something about why I reject it. Then, I will

---

1. The "health and wealth gospel" is also known as the "prosperity gospel," and the doctrines that support it are called "prosperity theology." There are some differences among different advocates of this doctrine. What follows is a summary statement which would be true of the teaching of most of the proponents of this theology. Information for this introduction, for the most part, derives from two internet articles: "How the Health and Wealth Gospel Twists Scripture," www.watchman.org/articles/other-religious-topics/how-the-health-and-wealth-gospel-twists-scripture/ and "5 Errors of the Prosperity Gospel" by David W. Jones, www.thegospelcoalition.org/article/5-errors-of-the-prosperity-gospel.

consider some New Testament passages that are used to support it.

What Is the Prosperity Gospel?

The prosperity gospel springs from the idea that God wants all His children to be both healthy and wealthy. It teaches that because of sin, people are poor and sick. Jesus came into the world to remedy that problem. His atoning death on the cross was intended (at least in part) to make it possible for people to overcome disease and poverty. Thus, the message of this perverted gospel is that all Christians deserve, and so should desire, to be rich. One of the forerunners of the health and wealth movement wrote, "It is not possible to live a really complete or successful life unless one is rich."[2]

Furthermore, according to this doctrine, if you want to be rich and healthy, you can. All you have to do is to believe, or have faith, and you will have whatever you want. Faith involves visualizing your goal and then laying claim to it. To claim it, all you have to do is name it! Confess it aloud, and it is yours! Since we are made in the image of God, and God could speak things into existence, so can we. If we speak it, it will be ours!

It also teaches that we are in a covenant relationship with God which obligates Him to do whatever we ask. To ask God in prayer for anything we want requires Him to give it to us—

---

2. Wallace D. Wattles, *The Science of Getting Rich* (Holyoke, MA: E. Towne, 1910), 9. Quoted by David W. Jones and Russell S. Woodbridge, *Health, Wealth & Happiness: Has the Prosperity Gospel Overshadowed the Gospel of Christ?* (Grand Rapids, MI: Kregel Publications, 2011), 44. Wattles is identified as one of the "New Thought" thinkers from whom past-day and present-day "prosperity preachers" have drawn their doctrines.

whether it is money we ask for or the healing of our bodies or anything else.

Furthermore, health and wealth advocates teach that God blesses us abundantly when we give—and especially when we give to the televangelist preaching the health and wealth gospel! We cannot out give God! So if we give $10 to Him, we can expect to receive, not just $10, or $100, but $1,000! These monetary blessings are assured; the followers of the doctrine are urged to keep track of what they get compared to what they give, and are told that if they do so they will always discover that they have received from God much more than they have given to Him.[3]

Connected to the promise of material prosperity which comes as a result of believers' covenant relationship with God, the doctrine says that believers will be healthy and rich, and they should live like it! God's children should go first class—designer clothes, fancy automobiles, expensive homes, etc. And those who preach this doctrine exemplify it by making sure that they live luxuriously off the gifts their faithful adherents send to them.

The appeal of this doctrine is obvious. Everyone wants to be healthy and wealthy. If we can get health and wealth at the same time that we get religion, so much the better! No wonder

---

3. My wife Sharlotte witnessed an example of this doctrine when she was watching "The 700 Club" show on television on September 28, 2015. The program that day told the story of a young couple who was having financial problems, so they decided to double their contributions to the 700 Club for four months. Two or three days after giving the fourth month's contribution they received two checks for $1,000 from a relative. Since then, nine years ago, according to the wife, they have continued giving their doubled contribution and her husband has received three promotions with raises in pay.

some of the largest churches in the United States have preachers who proclaim the health and wealth gospel.

But is this teaching true?

Misuse of the Prosperity of the Patriarchs

First, the health and wealth preachers mistakenly teach that since God made promises to Abraham, Isaac, and Jacob that resulted in their becoming wealthy (Gen 12:16; 13:2; 24:35; 26:13; 30:43), we can likewise expect to be blessed with abundant possessions today. They fail to see that the patriarchs had a unique role in the plan of God. They were the progenitors of the covenant people Israel, through whom the Promised Seed would come who would bring salvation to all mankind.

God's relationship with the patriarchs—including the material wealth He blessed them with—was not duplicated after their days. Thus, while Christians are the recipients of spiritual blessings which result from the promises made to Abraham (Gal 3:14), they are not promised the wealth and prominence enjoyed by Abraham.

Misunderstanding of Old Testament Promises

Second, the "prosperity preachers" wrongly apply the promises made to Israel in the Old Testament to Christians today. Thus, they say, since Israel was frequently promised material blessings for obedience, Christians can expect to be blessed in a similar way.

It is true that God promised the nation of Israel that He would bless them materially if they obeyed Him (and would curse them if they disobeyed Him). See, for example, Leviticus 26. However, we no longer live under the Old Testament (Heb 1:1-2; Gal 3:24-25; Eph 2:15), so even if there was the equivalent of a prosperity gospel in Old Testament days, it would not apply to us today. The Old Testament covenant promises were intended for the nation as a whole and not for every individual Israelite. The covenant was made with Israel (Exod 19), and according to that covenant if Israel (the nation) obeyed, God would bless the nation; if Israel (the nation) disobeyed, God would curse the nation. Old Testament history demonstrates how God fulfilled both His threats and His promises to the nation.

Since the covenant promises were made to the nation as a whole, there was no guarantee that righteous individuals would be either healthy or wealthy. In fact, numerous Old Testament scriptures give evidence that sometimes the righteous experienced poverty or suffering and the wicked prospered (Hab 1:4, 13; Psa 37:16, 17; 73:3-14; Jer 12:1; Prov 16:8).[4] The fact that there can be righteous people who are poor, or righteous people who suffer, nullifies the health and wealth theory.

So when Malachi says, "'Bring all the tithes into the storehouse ... And try Me now in this,' says the Lord of hosts, 'If I will not open for you the windows of heaven and pour out for you such blessing that there will not be room enough to receive it'" (Mal 3:10),[5] God is not stating an unbreakable law, true for all ages. He is simply restating the covenant law of blessings

---

4. The Old Testament contains examples of good men who suffered (Job; Naboth, 1 Kings 21:11-14), and of those who were diseased through no fault of their own—and who were not healed by God (Mephibosheth; see 2 Sam 4:4).

5. Quoted from the New King James Version. Unless otherwise indicated, all Bible quotations will be taken from the NKJV.

Introduction

and curses found in the Pentateuch. If Israel, as a whole, obeyed the law and gave what it was supposed to give, then the people as a whole would be blessed by God.[6]

Misrepresentation of Christ's Purpose

Third, the "health and wealth" teachers misrepresent the purpose of Christ's coming. God did not send His Son to make people healthy and wealthy but that "whoever believes in Him should not perish but have everlasting life" (John 3:16). Jesus said that He came "to seek and to save that which was lost" (Luke 19:10); and Paul wrote, "Christ Jesus came into the world to save sinners" (1 Tim 1:15). God's primary concern in sending His Son, and Jesus' primary mission in coming to the earth and dying on the cross, was the salvation of souls, not the elimination of disease or the generation of wealth.

Mistaken View of New Testament Healing

Fourth, the practitioners of the "prosperity gospel" misunderstand the purpose of the healing ministry of Jesus and the

---

6. Old Testament passages which appear to promise material blessings to individuals for obeying the Lord (such as Psalm 1 and Psalm 128) need to be read in the light of other passages which make it clear that those who are righteous do not always prosper. They should, therefore, be seen as stating a general principle: It is always better for the individual to obey the Lord. One writer made the same point as follows: "wisdom literature [such as that found in the book of Proverbs] ... provides only generalizations of what is often true." (Craig L. Blomberg, "Wealth," *The Baker Theological Dictionary of the Bible*, ed. Walter A. Elwell [Grand Rapids: Baker, 1996], 814.)

apostles.[7] They did perform miraculous acts of healing, but the primary purpose of these miracles was to convince humankind, both then and now, that Jesus was the Son of God and the message of the apostles was from heaven (John 20:30–31). Miraculous healing, along with other miracles, was used to confirm the word of the apostles—to attest that the message they spoke was from God (Mark 16:20; Heb 2:3–4).

In performing miracles of healing, Jesus and His followers demonstrated God's compassion for hurting people, but the main purpose of those miracles was to prove Jesus' divinity. Such miracles may also have served as a visual aid to help people understand that God could "heal" them spiritually, but their primary purpose was to make it evident that the Divine Messiah had come into the world, the prophesied Kingdom of God was near, and salvation was available!

That this sort of healing was not one of the primary objectives of Christ's coming is evident from the fact that not everyone was healed during the days of Christ and the apostles. Even Paul had to experience a "thorn in the flesh" (2 Cor 12:7–9). Timothy was afflicted with "frequent infirmities" (1 Tim 5:23). Paul left Trophimus "in Miletus sick" (2 Tim 4:20).

---

7. In this connection, the health and wealth practitioners misuse Isaiah 53:5, which includes the prediction regarding the Messiah: "By His stripes we are healed." They use this passage to say that Jesus died on the cross to make physical healing available. A better understanding of the verse is that the "healing" it speaks of is spiritual healing: through Jesus' death we can be healed of our spiritual sickness. That this is the correct interpretation is evident from the fact that 1 Peter 2:24 speaks of Christ bearing "our sins in His own body on the tree," and then indicates that by doing so Jesus fulfilled the prophecy "by whose stripes you were healed."

We conclude therefore that miracles of healing, like the other miraculous gifts, were part of the infancy of the church, and that they, like the other miraculous gifts, are no longer available for Christians today.[8]

Rejection of Christ's Teaching About Riches and Poverty

Fifth, "health and wealth" preachers deliberately ignore or deny Jesus' negative teachings about riches.

Jesus Himself provided an example of an obedient Israelite who lived as a poor man. He was born in a stable (Luke 2:7); when He was born, His parents offered the sacrifice reserved for the poor (Luke 2:24; Lev 12:6-8); He grew up in a despised town (John 1:46); He worked as a carpenter (Mark 6:3); He preached from a borrowed boat (Matt 13:1, 2; Mark 4:1); during His personal ministry He lived on the gifts of others (Luke 8:1-3); He was buried in a borrowed tomb (Matt 27:57-60); and apparently at the end of His life He owned nothing except the garments He wore to Golgotha (John 19:23-24).

Furthermore, Jesus obviously did not intend to make all His followers wealthy because most of what the Gospels have to say about wealth is negative.

- Mary predicted that with the coming of the Messiah "the rich" would be "sent away empty" (Luke 1:53); in contrast, Jesus pointed out that the coming of the Messiah meant

---

8. This is not to deny that God heals people today. In a sense, all healing is "divine healing," in that it comes from God. It is rather to deny that God heals people miraculously today as He did in the New Testament—as, for example, He did when Peter and John healed the lame man in Acts 3.

that the poor would be "blessed" (Luke 6:20) and would have the gospel preached to them (Luke 4:16–21).
- Jesus said that riches are "deceitful" and can result in the word sown in one's heart not bearing fruit (Mark 4:19).
- Jesus told His disciples not to lay up "treasures on earth" (Matt 6:19–21).
- Jesus said that it was "easier for a camel to go through the eye of a needle than for a rich man to enter the kingdom of God" (Matt 19:24).
- Jesus told the story of the rich man who stored up his "crops" and his "goods" so that he would have plenty for many years, but who died that night, to illustrate what it was like to lay up treasures for oneself when one was "not rich toward God" (Luke 12:15–21).
- Luke said that the Pharisees were "lovers of money" (Luke 16:14), and the Gospels unanimously affirm that, as a group, they were opponents of Jesus.
- In the story of Lazarus and the rich man (Luke 16:19–31), after death it is the poor man who is comforted and the rich man who is tormented.

How can one who is familiar with the life and teachings of Jesus still claim that He wants to make all His followers wealthy?

Failure to Account for Persecution

Sixth, those who proclaim the health and wealth gospel fail to recognize that Jesus Himself did not promise health and wealth to His followers, nor did any of the inspired New Testament writers.

Introduction

In fact, what Jesus promised to His disciples was that they would be persecuted! He told them that they would be blessed if they were persecuted (Matt 5:10-12). When He sent out the twelve apostles to preach to the Jews, He told them to expect to be persecuted (Matt 10:16-23). Just before He died He told them again that the world would "hate" them and persecute them (John 15:18-20).

Jesus' predictions came true, as is obvious in the book of Acts. The apostles were taken into custody and commanded not to preach in the name of Jesus (Acts 4 and 5). Stephen (Acts 7) and James (Acts 12) were martyred. Saul persecuted the church (Acts 8:1-3). Then the persecutor became the persecuted. The latter part of Acts is about Paul's preaching of the gospel to the Gentiles (as well as to the Jews), and his constant persecution by both Jews and Romans (for his account of his persecutions, see 2 Cor 11:23-26).

Christians throughout the Roman Empire were persecuted. Paul said that the Thessalonian church had been persecuted, had experienced tribulations, had suffered, and had been troubled (2 Thess 1:4-6). The churches to which Peter's first epistle was written were to expect a "fiery trial," which involved suffering (1 Pet 4:12-14). Peter consoled them with the words, "If anyone suffers as a Christian, let him not be ashamed, but let him glorify God in this matter" (1 Pet 4:15; see also v. 19).

In Revelation the picture of the saints in heaven is of some who came out of "the great tribulation" (Rev 7:14). Then after the New Testament era the pages of church history are stained red with the blood of martyrs.

Would an unbiased reader of the New Testament conclude that Christ came to give health and wealth to each of His disciples? What Christians are promised is not prosperity, but persecution! Paul wrote, "All who desire to live godly in Christ Jesus will suffer persecution" (2 Tim 3:12).

Invalid View of Prayer

Seventh, those who promote the health and wealth gospel falsely claim that God is obligated to answer every prayer of His faithful children.

The New Testament does teach that God answers prayer (see Matt 7:7-9, for instance), but it also teaches that, to be answered, our prayers must accord with God's will. If we make a request of God to spend it on our "pleasures" (say, on a fancy car or a more prestigious job), then "we ask amiss" and we will not receive what we ask for (Jam 4:3).

We need to remember that, though we are in a covenant relationship with God, He is not our servant, bound to fulfill our every desire. He is still the Almighty Lord, Ruler of everything, who knows and does what is best, even if we have asked for something else. The only prayer that God will guarantee to answer is, "Thy will be done" (see Matt 6:10; 26:39, 42).

Appeal to Unworthy Motives

Eighth, the health and wealth gospel is wrong because it appeals to wrong motives. The Bible says that the "love of money is a root of all kinds of evil" (1 Tim 6:10), but the prosperity gospel's appeal is directed towards humanity's desire for wealth. Its teachers urge people to give that they might get more. In contrast, Jesus taught His disciples to give to others "hoping for nothing in return" (Luke 6:35), and Paul urged Christians *not* to "desire to be rich" (1 Tim 6:9).

The health and wealth gospel is not the gospel taught in the New Testament. David W. Jones and Russell Woodbridge put it well:

> A study of the biblical teaching on wealth and poverty makes clear that the prosperity gospel is not the biblical gospel. Whereas the biblical gospel encourages people to work in order to meet their needs, the prosperity gospel emphasizes the conjuring of mystical forces of faith in order to meet material needs; whereas the biblical gospel stresses focusing on the material needs of others, especially those who are impoverished, the prosperity gospel focuses on acquiring wealth for oneself; and finally, whereas the biblical gospel warns people about the spiritual pitfalls of accumulated wealth, the prosperity gospel is consumed with the accumulation of wealth. The prosperity gospel is no gospel at all.

Christ's major concern—and the concern of the New Testament church—was lost souls. People steeped in sin needed (and need) to be saved. If we want to be like Christ, and operate as His church on earth, we too must make the saving of lost souls our primary business. Those who espouse the health and wealth gospel seem to be more interested in man's earthly welfare than in his spiritual wellbeing. Financial concerns are more important than saving souls.

Introduction

The prosperity gospel is easy to sell. Preachers who proclaim it are popular. However, their preaching so distorts the gospel that it has almost nothing in common with the gospel which is the power of God unto salvation (Rom 1:16). The fact that the doctrine they preach is popular does not make it right! Rather, it puts them into the category of false teachers who are in the business of scratching "itching ears" (2 Tim 4:3). It identifies them as false teachers who preach a gospel different from that preached by the apostles and received by those who heard them (Gal 1:8–9)!

Here's my advice. Don't listen to such preachers!

However, its preachers think that they find evidence for their teaching in the New Testament. What about the New Testament scriptures that are used by those who espouse "prosperity theology"? In light of what the New Testament as a whole teaches about wealth, it is obvious that the passages used to prove the health and wealth gospel are, in fact, misused. In this chapter, we want to consider some of those passages and briefly suggest why they do not support the health and wealth gospel.

NT Passages Used to Prove the Health and Wealth Gospel

Matthew 6:33: "All These Things Will Be Added to You."

Jesus said, "Seek first the kingdom of God and His righteousness, and all these things will be added to you" (Matt 6:33). In the context, this promise does not refer to riches, but to the necessities of life (what we have to eat or drink and what we have to wear).

Given the fact the New Testament teaches that Christians were to be persecuted, and that sometimes they were killed because of their faith, probably Jesus' promise should be understood to mean that if we do God's will, if we put Him first, He will give us what He thinks we need, not necessarily what we believe we have to have.

3 John 2: A Prayer for Prosperity and Health

To Gaius John wrote, "Beloved, I pray that you may prosper in all things and be in health, just as your soul prospers" (3 John 2). This is not a promise of wealth ("prosper in all things") and "good health" to Gaius, much less to anyone else, either of his day or ours. It is rather a conventional greeting, such as we might use if we begin a letter by saying, "I hope all is well with you."

David W. Jones and Russell Woodbridge agree with this position, writing that with this sentence John "is simply opening his letter with a greeting."[9] They add that the word "prosper" in the original Greek does not necessarily have anything to do with doing well materially, noting that various modern versions translate the passage without using the word "prosper." The NIV for example has, "that you may enjoy good health and that all may go well with you, even as your soul is getting along well." And the ESV translates, "that all may go well with you and that you may be in good health, as it goes well with your soul."[10]

---

9. Jones and Woodbridge, *Health, Wealth & Happiness*, 100.
10. Jones and Woodbridge, *Health, Wealth & Happiness*, 100.

Introduction

Matthew 9:29: "It Shall Be Done to You According to Your Faith."

In Matthew 9:29 Jesus healed two blind men by saying, "It shall be done to you according to your faith" (NASB). This passage is used to prove that Christians can have anything they want if they believe strongly enough.

The passage itself gives no evidence that Jesus was laying down a rule applicable to every situation for the rest of time. The most that can be said is that Jesus required faith for healing in this instance, though faith on the part of the person healed was not always a requisite for healing. To take a sentence out of its context and make it into an unbreakable rule is to misuse scripture.

John 10:10: The Abundant Life

In John 10:10 Jesus said that He came so that His "sheep" "may have life, and that they may have it more abundantly." Prosperity preachers assume that a Christian's having an "abundant life" must mean that he or she will have an abundance of earthly possessions. However, as many Christians can testify, the Christian life is the "abundant life" whether one has much or little of the world's goods. R.V.G. Tasker commented on this verse: "He [Jesus] does not offer them [His sheep, His disciples] an extension of physical life nor an increase of material possessions, but the possibility, nay the certainty, of a life lived at a higher level in obedience to God's will and reflecting His glory."[11]

Christians have an abundance of blessings: the forgiveness of sins, the Holy Spirit to dwell within them, Jesus Christ as their mediator, God as their Father, a community of believers (the church) to support and encourage them, the assurance of divine providence working in their lives (Rom 8:28), the promise of answered prayer, the knowledge that God will provide a "way of escape" for every temptation (1 Cor 10:13), and the hope of heaven! No wonder the Christian life is the abundant life, whether one is rich or poor!

Mark 10:29-30: You Shall Receive "a Hundredfold"

According to Mark 10:29, 30, Jesus said, "Assuredly, I say to you, there is no one who has left house or brothers or sisters or father or mother or wife or children or lands, for My sake and the gospel's, who shall not receive a hundredfold now in this time—houses and brothers and sisters and mothers and children and lands, with persecutions—and in the age to come, eternal life." While this passage does make promises, it is obvious that they are not to be taken literally. No one, for instance, would argue that being a faithful Christian will lead to the literal multiplication of one's "mothers and children."

It should also be noted that whatever the positive promises refer to, they are to be accompanied by "persecutions." Thus, the promise of the passage is not a picture of undiluted health and wealth. Given what the Bible teaches elsewhere, Jesus'

---

11. *The Gospel According to St. John*, Tyndale New Testament Commentaries (Grand Rapids: Eerdmans, 1960, 1968), 130.

words should be interpreted to mean that anyone who gives up anything to serve the Lord will be blessed with far more than he gave up—not necessarily with material blessings but with spiritual blessings.[12]

Luke 6:38: "Give and It Will Be Given to You"

According to Luke 6:38, Jesus said, "Give and it will be given to you: good measure, pressed down, shaken together, and running over will be put into your bosom. For with the same measure that you use, it will be measured back to you."

Preachers of the health and wealth gospel take these words of Jesus literally to mean that "you cannot out give God." The more money you give, the more money God will make sure you have. The problem with that interpretation is that it is hard to reconcile with the rest of the New Testament which teaches that sometimes even the most faithful Christians will suffer rather than prosper, in spite of how much they have given.

---

12. Jesus' words are addressed specifically to the apostles who had reacted with wonderment at Jesus' reply to the rich young ruler. Jesus' negative remarks concerning riches cause them to ask what they will receive since they have left everything to follow Jesus (Mark 10:28). Jesus' promise, therefore, is best applied to those who, like the apostles, give up what they have to spend their lives preaching the gospel. What is their reward? Persecution! But along with that persecution, hundreds of "brothers and sisters and mothers and children" *in the church*, with whom the preacher/missionary/teacher has as close a relationship as he does with his blood kin! Likewise lands (or "farms," NASB)—owned by his brothers and sisters in Christ, but which, on his travels, he can visit, which he can benefit from, and where he can feel as much at home as he did on his own "land" or "farm." The passage's primary application is not, therefore, to every Christian, but to those who are called to preach; and they are not promised either health or wealth in the usual sense of those terms.

One way to reconcile this teaching with other apparently contradictory passages is to assume that Jesus is talking about being blessed spiritually. The more you give—whether you give money or anything else (a kind word or a helping hand, for instance), you will be abundantly blessed by God with spiritual blessings (rather than material blessings). One thing that suggests this "spiritual" interpretation is that the previous verse is about forgiving and refusing to judge your fellow man. Perhaps the main message of v. 38 is that if you give your love to others—for example, by forgiving them and not judging them, God will bless you far more than you can imagine.

2 Corinthians 8:9: "You Might Become Rich"

In 2 Corinthians 8:9 Paul wrote, "For you know the grace of our Lord Jesus Christ, that though He was rich, yet for your sakes He became poor, that you through His poverty might become rich."

Proponents of the prosperity gospel take Paul's statement about becoming rich literally. Whatever Jesus did, He did so that the Christians at Corinth (and presumably others as well) might "become rich."

A more likely reading of the passage is that Paul is saying that Jesus "became poor" when He left heaven (see Phil 2:5–8) and that He did it for our sake, in order that we might "become rich" spiritually, having the abundance of spiritual blessings already mentioned in this chapter. Now since the Corinthians are rich spiritually, they should share their material possessions with the poor saints in Jerusalem—the primary message of 2 Corinthians 8 and 9. The passage, in other words, is not talking about Christ's making or promising to make the

Corinthians wealthy. Instead, it is challenging them to use whatever wealth they have for the cause of Christ, and it uses Christ's sacrifice in coming to earth and dying on the cross to bless them as one reason to do so.[13]

Conclusion

How does the proposition that faithful Christians are likely to prosper differ from the "health and wealth gospel"?

For one thing, we are not claiming that continuing prosperity is Christ's promise to every Christian; and we do not define "prosperity" as being equal either to health or to wealth.

For another, we are not urging people either to become Christians or to remain Christians primarily because of the prosperity they are likely to enjoy. Rather than seeing that prosperity as a motive, we see it as a result of faithful living, and as a blessing for which Christians can be grateful.

We do not serve the Lord to become prosperous, but we rejoice in whatever the Lord chooses to do for us. And we give thanks to Him for whatever He gives us—good or bad, little or much, pleasant or unpleasant. Our claim is simply that, generally speaking, under ordinary circumstances, a Christian is more likely to prosper than not, as a kind of by-product of living the Christian life.

---

13. Jones and Woodbridge say concerning this passage: "Paul is not saying that Christ died on the cross for the purpose of increasing one's material net worth. In fact, he is actually teaching the exact opposite. Contextually, it is clear that Paul was teaching the Corinthians that since Christ accomplished so much for them through the atonement, they ought to empty themselves of their riches in service of the Savior"; see Jones and Woodbridge, *Health, Wealth & Happiness*, 90.

Introduction

So what about the health and wealth gospel? Perhaps, to see its fallacies, one can imagine what a health and wealth preacher might have said or written, instead of what we find in the New Testament. If the apostles and New Testament evangelists believed the prosperity gospel, would they have said the following?

- Acts 2:38: "Repent, and let every one of you be baptized in the name of Jesus Christ for the remission of sins; and you shall receive" … "health and wealth."
- Matthew 5:10: "Blessed are those" … "who are not persecuted, but who lay claim to the goods they want by naming those goods."
- 2 Timothy 3:12: "All who desire to live godly in Christ Jesus" … "will be healthy and wealthy."
- Mark 16:15–16: "Go into all the world and preach" … "the good news of material prosperity to all creation. He that believes this gospel shall be both healthy and wealthy."
- 1 Timothy 6:10: "The love of money" … "is the beginning of wealth; love it, believe it, name it, and claim it; and riches will be yours. Longing for money has enriched many disciples, and it can make you wealthy, too."

I hope that reading these twisted versions of New Testament passages made you react negatively. I hope you exclaimed, "No, no, that's not what it says!" Nor is it what the New Testament means! Do not succumb to the siren call of the health and wealth gospel. It is false, fake, and foolish, and could cause you to forfeit your soul.

THAT ALL MAY GO WELL

PART 1

WHY CHRISTIANS PROSPER

When readers see that the subtitle of this book has to do with the prosperity of Christians, they might be tempted to look up the latest statistics to see how Christians in America fare financially compared to non-Christians—to people of other religions or to those who claim no religious affiliation. You might be shocked to discover that those who profess Christianity are not, statistically speaking, the most prosperous people in the United States. In fact, those classified as "evangelical protestants" are far down on the list based on their average annual income. (Hindus, Jews, and Greek Orthodox members top the list.)[1]

So how can I claim that Christians prosper? I could probably dispute the research methods used in the reported surveys, and/or question the conclusions that should be drawn from them. But instead I simply want to claim that this book is not about how those who believe in Christ as a whole are better off than anyone else. It's about how individual Christians can, and

---

1. "Income Distribution Within U.S. Religious Groups," Pew Research Center, www.pewforum.org/2009/01/30/income-distribution-within-us-religious-groups/.

should, do better because they follow Christian principles than they would do if they did not live by those principles. Evidence for that assertion is abundant in the lives of many disciples of Jesus.

Did you know that some faithful Christians are rich? Even though Jesus said that it was harder for a rich man to go to heaven than for a camel to go through the eye of a needle (Matt 19), there were some rich Christians in New Testament times (1 Tim 6). And there are some rich Christians today. More significant for most of us is the fact that many Christians today, though not rich, are doing well financially. For example, the eldership of a congregation in a small west Texas town is made up of four men—a bank president, a school superintendent, a pharmacist, and a businessman who probably employs more than a dozen people. Obviously all are successful and doing well materially. The same is true of hundreds and thousands of other Christians around the globe.

Why are these Christians prospering? My premise is that the prosperous Christian is not the exception but the rule. The thesis of this book is that Christians who do their best to obey the Bible are, under ordinary circumstances, more likely to prosper than they would if they were not faithful Christians.

Before you object that many good Christians are not prospering, and are, in fact, poor, let me clarify. Just being a Christian will not magically transport you from poverty to plenty. I believe that following the teachings of Christ will generally result in a Christian living a happier, more successful, and more prosperous life. And, by the way, I think the same thing is true for people who are not Christians. If, for some reason, an unbeliever decided to live by the precepts of Christ, I believe he or she would (in this life) be better off, and would live a happier more successful, and more prosperous life than if he or she chose to live in another way!² For example, a fellow member of the adult Bible Class I attend on Sunday morning told about an older man he used to drink coffee with at McDonald's. At the time, his friend was in his nineties and had lived an interesting life. He had, for instance, worked on the Golden Gate Bridge when it was being built and had seen several workers fall to their deaths on that job. He had been married to his wife for thirty years or so, and she had recently died. Even though he was an agnostic, and thus noncommittal when it came to believe in God, he had gone to church with his wife all those years. He told my friend that he appreciated the kindness with which my friend had treated him, saying that most Christians had nothing good to say to him or about him because of his agnosticism. When my friend complimented him on the fact that he lived a good moral life, and that he was kind and helpful to others, he responded, "I really believe that the way you Christians live is the best way to live, even if there is no God."³ He was right, of course. If even an agnostic or an atheist lives by Christian principles, he or she will be better off in this life for having done so.

---

2. This position can be defended theologically on the grounds that God's ethical and moral system has changed little since creation. It has always been wrong to murder and commit adultery and steal. Those sins were sinful even before they were forbidden by the Law of Moses. Therefore, people who live by what might be called this universal moral code—even if they do not accept Jesus Christ or worship the Lord God—are more likely to do well in this life than those who reject it.

3. From a telephone interview with Lewis Duncan, a member of the Hillcrest Church of Christ in Abilene, TX, Dec 1, 2015. In a similar vein, Dusty Rhodes, a successful trial lawyer, said, "The meanest criminals appreciate Christianity." Dusty Rhodes, interviewed by Coy Roper, Abilene, TX, Dec 13, 2015.

Under Ordinary Circumstances

I contend that "under ordinary circumstances" Christians are likely to prosper. I define "ordinary" as the kind of circumstances most of us enjoy in a free democratic and capitalistic society. If we had lived in the ancient Roman Empire when Christians were being persecuted, we probably would not have prospered. If we lived today in a society where Christians are being persecuted, we probably would not prosper. Or if Christians live today in extraordinary circumstances—when things are hard for everyone—during an extended drought, say, or a depression or recession—they, like everyone else, will probably suffer financially.

More Likely

I am not talking about an unbreakable rule. I am not saying that every faithful Christian will undoubtedly, inevitably, always, and forever prosper. I am rather talking about tendencies, about a "likelihood," about possibilities and probabilities. I am saying that generally speaking, more often than not, faithful Christians are likely to prosper. And I don't think we need to apologize for dealing with the subject in those terms. We all do a lot of things because we think that if we do them, the percentages are in our favor.

To Prosper

"Prospering" is not the same thing as "getting rich." I do not intend to imply that everyone who lives as a faithful Christian is likely to get rich as a result. "Prosperity" is a relative concept.

A citizen of Moody, Texas, who is regarded as "prosperous" might not have nearly as much money as a prosperous citizen of Beverly Hills. If we define "prosperity" in terms of material possessions, it takes a lot more to be thought of as "prosperous" in 2020 than it did, say, in 1935. What I am saying is that Christians are likely to prosper in the circumstances in which they find themselves. Christians who are small farmers will probably be relatively prosperous small farmers. Likewise, if they are school teachers, factory workers, business owners, plumbers, custodians, or police officers, they will be relatively prosperous—prosperous compared to others in similar circumstances in the community.

If They Were Not Faithful Christians

I am not saying that faithful Christians will necessarily prosper more than the person who invented Facebook. What I am saying is that they will do better than they would do if they did not try to live by God's rules.

In other words, I am not comparing a Christian's prosperity with a non-Christian's prosperity. Rather, I am comparing the prosperity of Christians to the prosperity they would have experienced if they had not been Christians or had not tried to live as Christians.

There are obviously many reasons why an individual might get rich. He or she might be born into a rich family or might have extraordinary talents. He or she might be exceptionally bright or might just get lucky.[4] (Christians, of course, believe that if they obtain wealth, it is because God has blessed them, for all good gifts come from God [Jam 1:17]). If a faithful

---

4. To use the word "lucky" in the way it is commonly used.

Christian was involved in an economic contest with people in these categories, he or she might come out way behind.

But the Christian has not entered such a contest! The only fair comparison is this. How well did an individual do compared to what that same individual might have done? On that basis, we affirm that faithful Christians will, as a rule, do better economically than they would have done if they were not faithful Christians.

Conclusion

So what am I talking about in the following pages? I am not talking about God's infallible promise to make every faithful Christian rich in this world's goods. There is no such promise in scripture. Rather, in western society, under ordinary circumstances, Christians who concentrate on doing God's will by obeying the Bible are likely to find themselves among the more prosperous people in their group. That fact is not, of course, the best reason for one to become a Christian or to live a faithful Christian life. The most important reasons to repent and turn to Christ, and then to live for Christ, are spiritual—to have forgiveness of sins, to become a child of God, and to go to heaven.

But the, perhaps surprising, fact that you are also likely to be blessed materially when you serve the Lord is like icing on the cake. It's a kind of serendipity, an added blessing, for which you can thank God. And if that fact encourages you, or someone else, to become a Christian and/or to live faithfully for Christ, so be it. May God be praised.

1

BECAUSE THEY WORK HARD

Having considered the false notions of the health and wealth gospel, I can still affirm that, generally speaking, Christians are likely to prosper—not that they will necessarily get rich, but that they will do relatively well in their own circumstances. Some research has tended to confirm this proposition. Studies have shown that practicing one's Christianity is likely to lead to a higher level of material prosperity and a greater sense of well-being. For example, one study discovered that "doubling the rate of religious attendance raises household income by 9.1 percent, [and] decreases welfare participation by 16 percent from base line rates."[1]

A scholarly paper on "Religion and Well-Being" said, "Most recent empirical work in the psychology of religion does indeed show that some aspect of religion (e.g. religious attendance or intrinsic religiosity) correlates positively with some index of well-being: Religious people report being

---

1. Linda Gorman, "Is Religion Good for You?," https://www.nber.org/digest/oct05/w11377.html. This article is basically a review of another: "Religious Market Structure, Religious Participation, and Outcomes: Is Religion Good for You?" by Jonathan Gruber.

happier and more satisfied with their lives."[2] Another study reached a similar conclusion: "Americans who are very religious have higher wellbeing than those who are less religious."[3]

Why do Christians usually prosper? In this chapter I want to consider one reason for their prosperity. THEY WORK HARD. One reason Christians are likely to do well, materially under normal circumstances, is that—if they obey God's word—they will be both industrious and wise as they work to make a living.

A willingness to work hard has traditionally been associated with prosperity. In fact, America's material wealth as a nation has, in part, been traced to a tradition which began with the first European settlers on the North American continent. The Pilgrims were religious and valued hard work and frugality—principles that became part of what might be called "the American way of life." Those principles helped shape America and contributed to its prosperity. Many will admit the beneficial influence of this tradition of hard work on this country without recognizing that the Pilgrim's view of work (called the "Puritan

---

2. Adam B. Cohen and Kathryn A. Johnson, "Religion and Well-Being," a paper presented at the Yale Center for Faith and Culture consultation on Happiness and Human Flourishing, sponsored by the McDonald Agape Foundation, https://faith.yale.edu/sites/default/files/cohen_and_johnson_0.pdf, p.1. In this article, the authors deal with a number of questions related to the subject, including possible reasons for the positive relation between religion and feelings of well-being.

3. Frank Newport, Dan Witters, and Sangeeta Agrawal, "Religious Americans Enjoy Higher Wellbeing," https://news.gallup.com/poll/152723/religious-americans-enjoy-higher-wellbeing.aspx.

work ethic" or the "Protestant work ethic") was derived from the Bible. Basically the Bible teaches three things about working.

Christians Must Work for a Living

Perhaps the first thing we should emphasize with regard to work is that Christians are required to work for a living. Writing to a church where, apparently, some had quit working (or were tempted to do so) because they expected the return of Jesus at any time, Paul said, "For even when we were with you, we commanded you this: if anyone will not work, neither shall he eat" (2 Thes 3:10).[4] It doesn't sound like the New Testament ethical system approves of the church supporting able-bodied people who intentionally refuse to work.

The message that God's people are to work is found in the Old Testament as well. Human beings were created to work (Gen 2:15); the sin of Adam and Eve caused their work to be harder (Gen 3:17–19), but work itself was not one of the curses resulting from the Fall. The book of Proverbs extols the virtue of hard work, and condemns laziness (the following verses are quoted from the NASB):

- 10:4—"Poor is he who works with a negligent hand, but the hand of the diligent makes rich."

---

4. See also Ephesians 4:28: "Let him who stole steal no longer, but rather let him labor, working with his hands what is good, that he may have something to give him who has need." According to this verse, one should work in order to have something to share with those in need.

- 12:27—"A lazy man does not roast his prey, but the precious possession of a man is diligence."
- 13:4—"The soul of the sluggard craves and gets nothing, but the soul of the diligent is made fat."
- 14:23—"In all labor there is profit, but mere talk leads only to poverty."
- 15:19—"The way of the lazy is as a hedge of thorns, but the path of the upright is a highway."
- 18:9—"He also who is slack in his work is brother to him who destroys."
- 19:15—"Laziness casts into a deep sleep, and an idle man will suffer hunger."
- 20:4—"The sluggard does not plow after the autumn, so he begs during the harvest and has nothing."
- 21:25—"The desire of the sluggard puts him to death, for his hands refuse to work."
- 24:33, 34—"A little sleep, a little slumber, a little folding of the hands to rest, then your poverty will come as a robber and your want like an armed man." (See also 24:30-32.)
- 28:19—"He who tills his land will have plenty of food, but he who follows empty pursuits will have poverty in plenty."

According to the Old Testament, the smart thing to do is to work for a living, rather than to be lazy. So the first message the Bible gives to one who wants to succeed is simply: Work. Work hard! Work diligently!

Christians Should Be Model Employees

The New Testament also teaches that Christians should work hard for their employers. What it says to Greco-Roman slaves might best be applied today to employees. Listen then to what God has to say to those who work for others:

> Servants, be obedient to those who are your masters according to the flesh, with fear and trembling, in sincerity of heart, as to Christ; not with eye service, as men-pleasers, but as servants of Christ, doing the will of God from the heart, with good will doing service, as to the Lord, and not to men, knowing that whatever good anyone does, he will receive the same from the Lord, whether he is a slave or free. (Eph 6:5–8)

> Servants, obey in all things your masters according to the flesh, not with eye service as men-pleasers, but in sincerity of heart, fearing God. And whatever you do, do it heartily, as to the Lord and not to men, knowing that from the Lord you will receive the reward of the inheritance; for you serve the Lord Christ. But he who does wrong will be repaid for the wrong which he has done, and there is no partiality. (Col 3:22–25)

Servants, be submissive to your masters with all fear, not only to the good and gentle, but also to the harsh. (1 Pet 2:18)

Let as many servants as are under the yoke count their own masters worthy of all honor, so that the name of God and His doctrine may not be blasphemed. And those who have believing masters, let them not despise them because they are brethren, but rather serve them because those who are benefited are believers and beloved. Teach and exhort these things. (1 Tim 6:1–2)

What does the Lord say to employees today?

- Work hard (or "heartily") for your employers, whether they are present or absent. Work as diligently for them as you would for Jesus if He were your employer. Don't try to take advantage of your employer.
- Be respectful of your employers. Be "submissive." Give them the honor due to them because of their position. Display a good attitude towards your employer.
- Do these things if your employer is harsh, even if you feel he or she does not deserve your respect.
- If you work hard, your employer (and others) will think well of Christianity; another reason is that Jesus Himself will reward you—not

necessarily with monetary gain but with His spiritual blessings.

If you bought a book on how to succeed at work, its rules could probably be summarized in the requirements found in the verses above.

Christians Should "Work Smart"

Sometimes we hear the advice: "Don't work harder; work smarter." The biblical advice is actually advice about working smarter. For the employee, for instance, it is smart to be respectful. Many times, employees are tempted to be rude, smart-alecky, and disrespectful towards their bosses, especially when they think their bosses are not worthy of respect.

The boss tells them to do something and they don't like it, so they respond to his or her order sharply and disrespectfully, maybe even with cutting humor. From the encounter they may get the satisfaction of knowing they have refused to be disrespected, and they have made their friends laugh. But they may also have gotten themselves fired! Is that the way to succeed? No! Rather, the smart thing to do is to respect, honor, and obey the boss.

Sometimes we don't work for others, but we work for ourselves. And sometimes we have others who work for us. Does the biblical work ethic have anything to say to us in such circumstances? For one thing, it basically tells us to get our lazy bodies out of bed and get to work!⁵ The passages quoted from Proverbs mostly relate to a farmer who decides for himself whether he will get out of bed and go to work each day. The message is when you work for yourself you will work diligently at your job (rather than sleeping late or failing to plant or cultivate your crops when it is time to do so)! Your diligence will then be rewarded. For another, the New Testament has something to say to masters (employers) as well as to slaves (employees). Notice Ephesians 6:9. "And you, masters, do the same things to them, giving up threatening, knowing that your own Master also is in heaven, and there is no partiality with Him." Consider also Colossians 4:1. "Masters, give your servants what is just and fair, knowing that you also have a Master in heaven."

Thus, Christian masters (employers) are required to treat their servants (their employees): (1) with consideration, recognizing that Christ is the Master of both employers and employees; (2) with justice and fairness; (3) with the understanding that one day Christ will call them to account for their actions. My point is this. *It is smart for employers to treat their employees well,* just as the Bible requires! If you're the boss, and if you want hardworking, loyal employees, then be fair, just and compassionate! That's the right thing to do; but we're

---

5. After my (third) retirement, I began a "career" as a free-lance writer. I now tell people that I am my own boss. Then I go on to say, "I have a lot of problems with my employee—I can't get him to work on time; he wants to be lazy on the job, to do as little as possible, to waste his time, to take too many naps. I think I'm going to have to cut his salary." One who hopes to succeed as a free-lance writer needs to find a solution to such problems.

saying it's also the smart thing to do, because it will result in employees who work harder and stay longer at their jobs, with the result that you are more likely to make a greater profit from your business.

Hard Work Will Help You Succeed

If you follow these biblical teachings concerning your work, will you be more, or less, likely to succeed, and thus to prosper? The answer is obvious. Employers are looking for loyal employees, with good attitudes, who work hard and always do their best for the business. Likewise, Christians who work for themselves or who are employers are more likely to do well if they follow biblical precepts than if they don't.[6] I can imagine the reader objecting, "But I—or someone I know—was the hardest worker in the company, and I—or he or she—still got laid off!"

If it seems that the rule that hard work helps you succeed isn't true in your case, remember:

- We are talking about a general principle, a general rule, not a rule without exceptions. Generally speaking, a person who works hard on a job is more likely to succeed at that job than one who doesn't. Since this is a general rule, there will be

---

6. The Bible teaches that if we work hard we are likely to do well in life. As Jones and Woodbridge observe, "The book of Proverbs teaches that hard, diligent work can lead to prosperity," *Health, Wealth & Happiness*, 164.

exceptions to the rule.

- We are also talking about ordinary circumstances. Sometimes extraordinary circumstances (such as a once-in-a-lifetime recession) can cause one to lose a job.
- Since human beings are both fallible and unpredictable, if one's continued employment depends on another human being, in this imperfect world employees are always subject to the malicious or arbitrary acts of those who are their superiors. No doubt hard workers sometimes lose their jobs through no fault of their own.

However, even if one who works hard for his or her boss loses a job, that employee is likely to get another job before long, and, being a hard worker, to succeed at that job.[7]

In other words, I believe that if you consider the "big picture," you will agree that the person who follows the biblical advice to work hard (and smart) for a living will, *in the long run*, be more likely to prosper than one who does not.

---

7. God does not, of course, guarantee that we will get the exact job that we are looking for in the exact place where we want to live. Some who remain unemployed do so because they refuse to lower their standards and work at a more menial job, or because they insist on getting a job in a certain location. Christians need to remember that the Bible requires them to work for a living; self-chosen unemployment for an extended period of time would not seem to be a viable option for one who seeks to do the will of God.

Hard Work—Part of a Balanced Life

However, the admonition to work hard should be qualified by the need to live a balanced life. Some people are inclined to overdo work, to become "workaholics," to be addicted to work. Consequently, they neglect their family, ruin their health, have no social life, forget their civic responsibilities, and starve themselves spiritually—all so that they can work longer hours to make more money. The Lord expected people to work, but He never intended for work to become humankind's goal and god; it was rather to be a means to an end—the means by which people supported themselves and their families and offered sacrifices to God.

While we are required by the Bible to work, our work must be secondary to other, more important, responsibilities, such as:

- Our responsibility to worship God and serve Him.
- Our responsibility to keep ourselves pure and be the "light of the world."
- Our responsibility to our family—especially the responsibility to be good spouses and parents. Children need their parents' physical presence—just as much, or more, than they need the money they make.
- Our responsibility to take care of our physical and mental health.

If we work so hard or for so many hours as to neglect these responsibilities, our lives are out of balance. Then, we need to stop, make adjustments, and start over.

Conclusion

Obviously, what I have just said is not the health and wealth gospel. I have not said that if you think right, you will get rich. I have not said that if you visualize yourself as having riches, they will come to you. This message is not as appealing. It is simply the old-fashioned admonition: If you work hard (and smart), you are likely to succeed in life.

This message comes, however, not from humanity, but from God. He teaches us in His Book to work hard. We should do so simply because He tells us to. If we do, as a by-product of our obedience, we will most likely do well in this life. The con-tinuing validity of the premise that hard work will help you succeed—as will good homes and a healthy life style—was sug-gested in the following paragraphs by columnist Cal Thomas:

> Need a plan for success, or at least independent living? It isn't new ... Get married before you have children, stay married and if things get tough seek counseling. Stay in school. Don't take

drugs. Develop good character and a sound work ethic ... The old values worked.[8]

Those "old values" are values which can be equated with the way of life required of Christians. They are the values I am recommending in this book.

---

8. Cal Thomas, "Restore old values; they worked," article on the "Opinion Page" of the *Abilene Reporter-News*, Abilene, TX, October 27, 2015, p. 6A.

2

BECAUSE THEY OBEY THE LAW

Crime is a costly enterprise. Its prevention, detection, and punishment are enormously costly for society. The fear of becoming a victim of crime prompts people to spend money on home security measures and often robs them of their peace of mind. Criminal acts extract a horrendous cost from their victims, who are likely to lose their property, experience bodily harm, and maybe even be killed. It also costs the perpetrators, who suffer serious consequences when they are caught and convicted of their crimes.[1] Christianity does not promise to eradicate criminal behavior from the world. What Christianity does for its adherents is to spare them from the expenses incurred by criminals. It keeps them from committing crimes. The result is that Christians are more likely to prosper than lawbreakers.

So, a second reason Christians are likely to prosper is that they are required by Scripture to obey the law of the land. I want to consider that biblical requirement and then think

---

1. Committing a crime is likely to result in the criminal's being fined and/or incarcerated. Even if some wrongdoers escape any significant punishment for crimes, they carry with them a criminal record—a significant deterrent to success.

about its consequences for Christians in today's world.

Obedience as a Biblical Requirement

The assertion that Christians are required to obey the law might come as a surprise. The world in general is a sinful place, and the rulers of the Roman Empire—the setting for New Testament events and writings—were often guilty of atrocities. The laws of the empire sanctioned acts which we certainly would consider immoral (such as slavery).

Furthermore, Christians were taught that they were not of this world, and that they owed their primary allegiance to a higher authority—to God Himself! Or to King Jesus! Why, then, we would wonder, should they have been required to obey the sinful, disreputable, rulers of the Empire? In fact, Christians were frequently accused of refusing to submit to legal authorities. Their opponents often sought reasons to charge Jesus and His disciples with breaking the law. For example, hoping to find fault with Him, some of Jesus' enemies asked if it were right to pay taxes to Caesar. His response was, "Render therefore to Caesar the things that are Caesar's, and to God the things that are God's" (Matt 22:21; see v. 15–22). In other words, Jesus taught that His disciples should pay the taxes due the civil authorities.[2] Again, when Jesus was tried, he was falsely accused of claiming to be a king in opposition to Caesar (John 19:12)—an accusation which contributed to Pilate's

---

2. Jesus also miraculously provided the "temple tax" for Himself and Peter (Matt 17:24–27). This tax was not imposed by Rome, but was paid yearly by each Jew to the priests and was used for the maintenance of the Temple in Jerusalem. See Sellers S. Crain, *Matthew 14–28, Truth for Today Commentary*, ed. Eddie Cloer (Searcy, AR: Resource Publications, 2011), 118–119.

decision to crucify Him, but a false accusation since Jesus made it clear that His kingdom was "not of this world" (John 18:36).

Similarly, the apostles and evangelists in the book of Acts were frequently accused of breaking the law. They were accused of causing trouble or dissension wherever they went; of teaching things which were unlawful; of proclaiming "another king, Jesus," which was contrary to Caesar's decrees; and of blaspheming local deities (Acts 16:20, 21; 17:6–7; 18:13; 19:23–40; 24:5). Paul was even mistaken for an Egyptian leader of a revolt (21:38). Christians denied these accusations. Paul's response to charges against him is probably typical: "Neither against the law of the Jews, nor against the temple, nor against Caesar have I offended in anything at all" (Acts 25:8). Though they were accused of being rebels and revolutionaries, first century Christians obeyed the law. It was important that the charges of law-breaking be refuted because if the church was to grow and if its members were to influence society for good, they needed to, as Paul said, "if possible, so far as it depend[ed] on [them], be at peace with all men" (Rom 12:18, NASB). If they were locked up in jail, their opportunities for evangelism would be curtailed; if they were seen as criminals and crooks, they would have difficulty being "the light of the world" (Matt 5:14).

Therefore, the clear teaching of the inspired apostles is that Christians are to obey the law of the land. Notice the following scriptures:

> Let every soul be subject to the governing authorities. For there is no authority except from God, and the authorities that exist are appointed by God.

Therefore whoever resists the authority resists the ordinance of God, and those who resist will bring judgment on themselves. For rulers are not a terror to good works, but to evil. Do you want to be unafraid of the authority? Do what is good, and you will have praise from the same. For he is God's minister to you for good. But if you do evil, be afraid, for he does not bear the sword in vain; for he is God's minister, an avenger to execute wrath on him who practices evil. Therefore you must be subject, not only because of wrath but also for conscience' sake. For because of this you also pay taxes, for they are God's ministers attending continually to this very thing. Render therefore to all their due: taxes to whom taxes are due, customs to whom customs, fear to whom fear, honor to whom honor. (Rom 13:1–7)

Therefore submit yourselves to every ordinance of man for the Lord's sake, whether to the king as supreme, or to governors, as to those who are sent by him for the punishment of evildoers and for the praise of those who do good. For this is the will of God, that by doing good you may put to silence the ignorance of foolish men—as free men, yet not using your liberty as a cloak for vice, but as servants of God. Honor all people. Love the brotherhood. Fear God. Honor the king. (1 Pet 2:13–17)

Therefore I exhort first of all that supplications, prayers, intercessions, and giving of thanks be made for all men, for kings and all who are in authority, that we may lead a quiet and peaceable life in all godliness and reverence. For this is good and acceptable in the sight of God our Savior. (1 Tim 2:1–3)

What does the New Testament require of Christians regarding their country's governing authorities? (1) They must pray for them. (2) They must honor them. That is, they must give them the respect due them because of the office they hold. (3) They must obey them. Thus, they are required to obey the laws of the land. (4) They must pay their taxes.

Are there any exceptions to these requirements? Any reasons why a Christian would be allowed not to keep them? It is important to notice that the New Testament does not say that only righteous rulers and good laws must be obeyed. Generally, Christians are to honor and obey rulers and laws even if they dislike or disagree with them. I say "generally" because the New Testament provides one obvious exception to the rule. When the apostles were commanded not to preach in the name of Jesus (Acts 5:28), Peter and the apostles replied, "We must obey God rather than men" (Acts 5:29, RSV). All would accept Peter's statement as a binding example. Christians must always "obey God rather than men." What does Peter's statement require? In the context in Acts, it means that if governing authorities require us to disobey God, we must obey God and disobey them! If a law were passed that said you could not preach the gospel, you would have to disobey that law. If there were a law requiring you to murder, steal, or commit adultery, you would have to disobey that law. Otherwise, we are to obey the laws of the land.

Blessed by Obedience

The point I want to stress is that if we obey God by obeying the laws of the land, we will be blessed—and we will be more likely to prosper than if we do not. That fact should be obvious. Who are the people in any community who could be thought of as the least prosperous? It's not really the homeless or destitute. It's the people in prison. I imagine that most in jail would gladly trade places with almost anyone on the outside, even someone who is poverty-stricken. No one wants to lose his or her freedom and go to jail. But that's where lawbreakers are likely to end up.

Even if the laws we break don't send us to jail, it is likely that our law-breaking will cost us something, in time or money. I heard of a man who objected to the seat belt law in his state. So, he refused to wear a seat belt when he drove his vehicle. The result was that he had paid, over the years, maybe fifty tickets for driving without wearing a seat belt. Consequently, he had the satisfaction of knowing that he had not bent his self-determined values to the will of the state; but his stubborn refusal to obey the law had also cost him hundreds of dollars. One wonders—is that smart?[3]

---

3. Some of us seem to be born with a contrary streak, a rebellious spirit. It pains us to be subservient to anyone, and it's especially difficult to honor someone we have come to despise. And there are laws that, to us, make no sense, or that violate what we see as our natural-born rights. It is hard, therefore, for us to submit to authorities and to obey their laws. Nevertheless, it is smart to follow God's law which says that we must obey civil law unless that law makes us disobey divine law. We would therefore be better off to quash our rebellious (or independent) spirit, at least to the point that we pray for, honor, and obey those in authority.

Sometimes—maybe even most of the time—lawbreakers think, "I won't get caught." They could be right. But usually they are wrong. Even if they are not caught immediately, they are likely to live an uncomfortable life from that time on, looking over their shoulder, as it were, imagining that the law is about to catch up with them. Furthermore, even if they get away with their crime, they have to live with a guilty conscience.[4] In the long run, and in general, crime does not pay! And the opposite is also true. In society in general, it is the law-abiding citizens who honor those in authority who are more likely to succeed, and therefore to prosper.

And those who are religious are more likely to be law-abiding citizens. Studies show that being religious makes one less likely to break the law. One internet article said, "Can religion help reduce violent crime? Two studies suggest the answer is yes, both by creating a moral climate that fosters respect among neighbors and by helping to form individual consciences of young adults."[5]

---

[4]. I believe this to be the rule. Most people have a conscience, and knowing that they have broken the law and done something that is seriously wrong (not just by driving too fast, for example) will leave them feeling guilty even if they do not get caught. Some people (fortunately only a few) seemingly have no conscience.

[5]. David Briggs, "Studies: Religion linked to fewer violent crimes; being 'spiritual but not religious' tied to increased risk," http://blogs.thearda.com/trend/featured/studies-religion-linked-to-fewer-violent-crimes-being-'spiritual-but-not-religious'-tied-to-increased-risk/.

Apparent Exceptions

Some may disagree with the premise that Christians obey the law and are therefore likely to prosper. Two objections are possible. One cannot disagree with this assertion. I have been talking about what the Bible requires. Christians, being human, will always fall short of the ideal. We all sin (1 John 1:8, 10). Sometimes Christ's disciples give in to temptation and break the law in significant ways. When they do, they, like everyone else, need to pay the penalty society imposes for committing a crime. The good news is that, whatever sin we are guilty of—no matter how terrible—we can be forgiven if we will turn to Christ by repenting of our sin and praying for forgiveness (Acts 8:22). Christians who have broken the law, and who have spent time in jail, can still be useful in God's kingdom if they truly repent.[6] Our point is that most Christians most of the time (not all Christians all the time) obey the law, with the result that Christians usually prosper.

Criminals don't always get caught and sometimes get rich. It may be that television programs and movies give us the impression that most "bad guys" "get away with it" and end up living "sumptuously every day"! My guess is that the truth is that most of those who commit crimes are caught and suffer consequences for their crimes. And even if criminals immediately escape punishment, most live impoverished lives. If

---

6. Likewise, it is possible for criminals who have never known Christ to turn to Him and be saved if they will believe in Christ and obey the gospel. When they do, Christ completely absolves them of all their sins; and they are spiritually free to begin life anew. Many former criminals have become Christians even while they were in prison, and when they were released they have served the Lord faithfully.

people commit crimes and think they "got away with it," that fact will probably encourage them to commit other crimes until they do get caught. Only in very rare cases are people who commit crimes likely to prosper. If they do, they do so at the expense of others who suffer because of their crimes.

Of course, the Christian knows that even if some people never have to pay for their crimes here, there will be a time when they pay for their crimes and sins hereafter. Even if earthly authorities never find out about certain criminal activities, there is One who knows about them—and He, the Lord God, will call people to account someday. If you do not fear judges and juries here, you need to learn to fear that Heavenly Tribunal where you will be judged someday. If one looks carefully at the potential "costs and benefits" of a life of crime, compared to the "costs and benefits" of a life in which one works for a living, it is unlikely that anyone in his or her right mind would choose to become a criminal.

Conclusion

If we lived in a time or place where Christianity was outlawed, Christians would probably not prosper; if we insisted on practicing our faith, we would probably end up in jail, or end up dead! Being a faithful Christian gives us an advantage because it is likely to keep us out of jail, and contribute to our becoming productive law-abiding citizens.

3

BECAUSE THEY PRACTICE CHRISTIAN VIRTUES

A third reason Christians prosper is simply that they, personally and individually, display Christian characteristics. They practice Christian virtues. In other words, they act like Christians! Is there such a thing as a Christian personality? Are all Christians alike? The answer is both "No" and "Yes"!

How Christians Are Not Alike

The answer is "No," in that some Christians are more introverted and some are more extroverted; some are governed more by logic and some are given more to emotional responses; some tend to see the "big picture" and others are more interested in the details of a plan and so forth.

These differing characteristics can be related to the different spiritual gifts which God has given different Christians (see Rom 12:3–7). We are not all made alike. Our ancestry and our experiences have made us different.

How Christians Are Alike: They Practice Christian Virtues

But the answer is also "Yes," in that Christians are required by their Lord to share some characteristics. No matter what kind of personality we have, or what spiritual gifts we have received, we are all to be alike in that we are all required, to the best of our ability, to take upon ourselves Christian virtues. What virtues? The complete answer to that question is found in the totality of God's word. Let's look at some of the passages which speak of virtues which Christians are required to practice.

Jesus Himself said that the main thing that ought to characterize His disciples is love: "By this all will know that you are My disciples, if you have love for one another." (John 13:35) The love that Christians should exhibit produces other virtues. As Paul said, "Love is patient, love is kind and is not jealous; love does not brag and is not arrogant, does not act unbecomingly (is not "rude," CEV), ... does not seek its own [is not selfish], is not provoked ("is not quick tempered," CEV) ..." (1 Cor 13:4, 5a, NASB)

There are other ways of listing the virtues Christians should possess. Jesus Himself mentioned some of those virtues when He said, among other things, that the "poor in spirit" (perhaps referring to those who are humble) and the "meek" and the "merciful" and the "pure in heart" and the "peacemakers" would be blessed (Matt 5:3, 5, 7–9). Another way of describing the characteristics of Christians is to speak of them as the "fruit of the Spirit," which consists of "love, joy, peace, longsuffering, kindness, goodness, faithfulness, gentleness [and] self-control" (Gal 5:22–23a). Then there are also lists of virtues required of Christians in the epistles, such as these commands found in Ephesians 4: "Speak truth each one of you with his neighbor ... Be angry and yet do not sin ... He who steals must steal no longer ... Let no unwholesome word proceed from your mouth ... Let all bitterness and wrath and anger and clamor and slander be put away from you, along with all malice. Be kind to one another, tender-hearted, forgiving each other just as God in Christ has forgiven you" (Eph 4:25–32, NASB; see also Col 3:12–14). And Peter urged Christians to "add to their faith" (KJV) the following virtues: knowledge, self-control, perseverance, godliness, brotherly kindness, and love (2 Pet 1:5–7). Finally, Jesus said that the second greatest commandment was to "love your neighbor as yourself" (Matt 22:39), and summed up our responsibility towards others with the words: "Whatever you want men to do to you, do also to them" (Matt 7:12a). We commonly paraphrase the command, "Do unto others as you would have them do unto you." What would it look like if a Christian practiced these virtues? He or she would:

Be loving	Rather than jealous, hateful, spiteful, malicious, wrathful, bitter, angry.
Be merciful	Rather than judgmental, condemning
Be a peacemaker	Rather than a warmonger, pugnacious, always spoiling for a fight
Be kind	Rather than cruel, cold, uncaring
Be selfless	Rather than selfish, self-centered
Be self-controlled	Rather than undisciplined
Be patient	Rather than quick-tempered

Be courteous	Rather than rude
Be gentle	Rather than being mean or threatening
Be humble	Rather than arrogant, rather than being a braggart
Be forgiving	Rather than holding grudges
Be joyous	Rather than dreary, somber
Be truthful	Rather than lying
Speak words that build up	Rather than words that tear down, or words of gossip or slander
Persevere	Rather than quitting when "the going gets tough"
Do good to all	Rather than seeking to hurt any one

The Benefits of Living Like a Christian

So here's the question. If Christians do their best to practice the characteristics Christ recommends, will they be—in this life—better off or worse off? One can imagine situations in which practicing Christian virtues would put disciples at a disadvantage. For instance, if you want to succeed in an organization dedicated to breaking the law, it is unlikely that being humble or being a peacemaker or being gentle would help you get ahead. But in most circumstances, it seems obvious that the person who could be described by the terms in the left column above would be more likely to prosper than the person who has the characteristics in the right column. Don't get me wrong. I'm not saying that the main reason you should adopt a Christian lifestyle is so that you can do better financially. Why should you want to live as Christ directs?

- Because the Lord tells you to, and if you love the Lord you will want to obey Him (John 14:15).
- Because in seeking to internalize these characteristics, you are becoming more like your Savior (1 Pet 2:21) who died for you and more like the God who loves you (Eph 5:1).
- Because, as God's child, you need to live a righteous life to influence others for good (Matt 5:16).
- Because you should want always to "do the right thing" so that you can go to heaven; those who live contrary to God's word will not find themselves there (Rev 21:8).

The primary reason why you should try to live the Christian life is not for the material benefits you will receive as a result. Nevertheless, you are likely to receive such benefits as a kind of serendipity, a by-product, an added benefit, of living as the Lord wants you to live. Jones and Woodbridge made this point as follows: "Rather than claiming—as proponents of the prosperity gospel do—that material wealth is a barometer of spiritual wealth, it is better simply to recognize that on account of the moral traits that accompany spiritual wealth (industry, honesty, diligence, etc.), material wealth often follows."[1]

Is it really true that exhibiting Christian characteristics will help you succeed? I can imagine that some will object, "That's not how it works in real life. I try always to do what I should as a Christian, but others who are immoral and lie and cheat get promotions instead of me!" Or, "In my line of work, the people who are most sinful are most likely to get ahead." Or, "I tried living as a Christian, seeking to do the right thing, standing up for Christ, and the result was that I was persecuted, demoted, and fired!"

I will attempt to answer some of these objections in the second part of the book ("Why They Don't"). Suffice it to say for now that I am talking about a general rule, not an unbreakable rule. I am saying, usually if you practice Christian virtues, try to show love for others, always try to do the right thing, etc., you will do better in life than if you don't.

Is there any evidence for this assertion? First, it just makes sense. Think about it. Who would you rather deal with? Someone who is courteous or someone who is rude? Who would you rather hire? Someone who lies or someone who tells the truth? Who would you rather do business with? People who act as if they are interested in you? Or folks who are interested only in themselves? In other words, in most circumstances it obviously pays to act like a Christian. For instance, in a book on

---

1. Jones and Woodbridge, *Health, Wealth & Happiness*, 140.

screenwriting, the author, in dealing with the business of trying to sell a screenplay, wrote: "It pays ... to be a decent, respectful human being, even in the movie industry" and, "in Hollywood, as elsewhere, one's selfish best interest is served when he treats people humanely."[2] That's another way of saying that one will do better if he displays Christian virtues. Second, successful people, and those who have studied what it takes to be successful, have reached conclusions which are at least compatible with the virtues required of Christians. For example, among the qualities that help one succeed they mention are the following three traits.

Integrity or Good Character

Those who know something about what it takes to succeed speak of the need for integrity or honesty or good character. In an interview, one entrepreneur attributed his success, at least in part, to the fact that people know him to be a man of integrity.[3] One who advises people how to succeed wrote, "When we become known for this highly valued trait [integrity], our lives and our careers can flourish."[4] In an article titled "The 10 Most Important Personality Traits for Career Success," another author argued ethics was crucial. One needs to be an ethical

---

2. Richard Walter, *Essentials of Screenwriting* (New York: Plume, 2010), 318.

3. Kevin Batten, from an interview with Coy Roper, Abilene, TX, November 20, 2015. The subject of the interview was: "How has the practice of Christian principles helped—or hindered—you in your career?"

4. Marcel Schwantes, "3 Huge Reasons Why Integrity Is So Important," https://www.linkedin.com/pulse/three-biggest-reasons-why-leadership -integrity-so-marcel-schwantes/

person to succeed; he or she needs to exhibit "the quality of having and living by a code of sound moral principles."[5] In a similar list, another author listed "good character" among the traits that make one successful.[6]

Friendliness or Consideration of Others

"Experts" on success testify that to succeed one needs to be friendly, outgoing, kind, and considerate of others. One writer said that those who are likely to succeed are both "generous givers" and good listeners.[7] Another said that to be successful one needs to be a "listener," to be willing "to suspend [his or her] own agenda and deliberately and empathetically allow others to be heard" and included in his list of other important qualities one needs to succeed are the attributes of being "friendly" and being "relationship-oriented."[8]

In an interview, a successful ophthalmologist said, "I make a point of always treating my patients fairly and honestly. I treat patients the way I would want to be treated."[9] He

---

5. Tom Denhem, "The 10 Most Important Personality Traits for Career Success," https://blog.timesunion.com/careers/the-10-most-important-personality-traits-for-career-success/633/. In listing the next twenty important traits needed for success, he included being self-sacrificial and trustworthy.

6. Robert Chen, "30 Qualities That Make Ordinary People Extraordinary," https://www.embracepossibility.com/blog/qualities-highly-successful-people/.

7. Chen, "30 Qualities That Make Ordinary People Extraordinary."

8. Denham, "The 10 Most Important Personality Traits for Career Success."

9. Dr. Brett Teague, in an interview with Coy Roper, conducted in Abilene, TX, on December 10, 2015.

attributed this behavior—which has helped him succeed—to his practice of Christian principles. I also interviewed Bruce Davis, a successful retired college teacher and businessman, who owned and operated several retirement homes. He said that he made his money by taking businesses that were about to fail and making them profitable. He attributed his success to the way that he treated the people involved. Among the things he said were the following:

- "We treated everyone like family."
- "We treated our employees like friends. If we were successful, we wanted our employees to be successful, too. So we would pay them accordingly. When we left, they were sad to see us go. The result was that our employees treated our clients well."
- "I learned to treat seniors well. Also I have learned to protect seniors. I have had to fire various employees at different facilities—people who didn't treat people right.
- "We wouldn't ask people to do anything that we wouldn't do."
- "We were successful because of the way we treated the people."[10]

---

10. Bruce Davis, from an interview conducted by Coy Roper in Abilene, TX, on December 18, 2015. Dr. Davis also headed the Gerontology Department at Abilene Christian University from its beginning in 1986 until he retired from fulltime teaching in 1995.

Self-Control

Those who write about the subject say that self-control is an important characteristic of those who succeed. "Self-Discipline" is tenth on one list of "The 10 Most Important Personality Traits for Career Success;"[11] and "Self-Control" is included in a list of "30 Qualities That Make Ordinary People Extraordinary."[12]

Can Christian Principles Get in the Way of Success?

Nevertheless, there may be some situations in which being a Christian can get in the way of success. When I interviewed Dr. Ian Shepherd, a Professor of Economics at Abilene Christian University, I asked him, "How has the practice of Christian principles helped—or maybe hindered—you in achieving success?" He began with how it had hindered his success in Australia. In the Australian culture, if you were in the 'in crowd—composed of those who consider one another 'mates,'—it was expected that you would drink. When you didn't, you were made fun of. And you never became part of the 'in crowd.' Even though I worked hard, I probably would not have made it above middle management in that culture."[13]

---

11. Denham, "The 10 Most Important Personality Traits for Career Success."

12. Chen, "30 Qualities That Make Ordinary People Extraordinary."

13. Ian Shepherd, in an interview with Coy Roper, conducted in Abilene, TX, on December 10, 2015. Dr. Shepherd was born in Australia and moved to the United States in 1987 at the age of 30. He had a successful business career before he began teaching in college.

In such circumstances what should a Christian do? The easy way would be to bow to pressure and follow the crowd in the hopes of achieving greater success and prosperity. But Christians march to the beat of a different drummer. The path they have chosen is not the easy way. It is difficult and narrow, but it leads to life (Matt 7:13–14).

Therefore, ideally Christians will not compromise on matters of conscience. If that results in the loss of a job, or in having to settle for a lower-paying job, or if it requires that someone look for a new job or even to change occupations, they will say, "So be it," and then they will set out to discover what God has in store from that time on.

Conclusion

I conclude that we will more likely be successful in life—and therefore we are more likely to prosper—if we become the kind of people Christ wants us to be. Two more points need to be made.

First, Christian characteristics do not belong exclusively to Christians. Adherents of other religions—and people who practice no religion—can also be compassionate and kind and forgiving. If they are—if they do not believe but still practice what we are calling "Christian virtues"—they will receive, in this life, the same kind of rewards Christians receive from adopting those virtues.

Second, since we are all imperfect and sin (1 John 1:8–10), we need to realize that the best of us will sometimes fall short of being "all that we can be." None of us have always displayed, and none of us will ever succeed in always displaying, Christian attitudes. The good news for those in Christ is that when we do fall short, if we are doing our best to be what we are supposed to be, we are cleansed by the blood of Christ (1 John 1:7), and we can, as it were, get back up, dust ourselves off, and get back on track, trying our hardest to run the Christian race as it is set before us (Heb 12:1–2).

Then as we progress in the Christian life, we will discover the truth of the saying I have heard, "Christians are not sinless, but Christians sin less." We will, hopefully, sin less and less as we mature in Christ.

4

BECAUSE THEY ACT WISELY

Christians are sometimes thought of (or portrayed) as ignorant, stupid, or naïve in the ways of the world. Consequently, it is assumed that they will always come in second (or third or tenth) to the worldly people who know how to get what they want. On the contrary, I would argue that Christians are likely to get ahead because they act wisely in all circumstances.

Which is not to say that Christians exercise what James calls "earthly" wisdom (Jam 3:14–16) or what Paul calls the "wisdom of this world" (1 Cor 1:18–25; see also 1 Cor 2). A Christian would not necessarily be wise about how to cheat, or steal, or lie, or slander. If you wanted to know how to (metaphorically) stab a fellow worker in the back, you would not want to ask a faithful Christian how to do it. Nevertheless, Christians are advised to act wisely at all times.

Wisdom in the Book of Proverbs

Christians recognize that though the Mosaic laws are not binding on them (Gal 3:23–25), the Old Testament has value for them (2 Tim 3:16, 17; 1 Cor 10:11; Rom 15:4). This is especially true for the book of Proverbs which presents wise sayings that are as true today as they were when they were first written. Those proverbs were intended to help people succeed. One could say that the way of wisdom is the way to success. And the one thing they recommend more than anything else is simply: Act wisely. Get and practice wisdom.

Included in the teachings of Proverbs are the following, more or less randomly chosen, words of advice:

- One should seek to acquire wisdom and understanding. (4:5–9; 16:16)
- "The fear of the Lord is the beginning of knowledge;" wisdom comes from the Lord. (1:7; 2:6, 7)
- Wise men seek to live righteous lives. (3:5–7; 10:6; 20:7)
- It is wise to be generous. (11:24–26)
- Wise people are careful about their speech. (14:3)
- It is wise to consult with others about your plans. (15:22; 12:15)
- It is wise to listen to rebukes. (17:10; 12:1)
- Sometimes it is wise to keep your mouth shut. (17:28)[1]
- Wisdom suggests we should be careful about whom we confide in (23:9) and whom we hire (26:10).
- "A fool always loses his temper, but a wise man holds it back." (29:11; NASB)

---

1. Compare James 1:19b: "Let every man be swift to hear, slow to speak, slow to wrath."

Anyone who wants to succeed in life—and with God—would do well to read the book of Proverbs and try to put the axioms he or she finds there into practice.

Wisdom in the New Testament

Wisdom is also recommended in the New Testament. In fact, there are New Testament passages which both require Christians to act wisely and provide examples of such behavior.

First and foremost we need to listen to Jesus. He said to His disciples, "Behold, I send you out as sheep in the midst of wolves; so be shrewd as serpents and innocent as doves" (Matt. 10:16, NASB; see also the NIV). Or, as other versions say, "Be wise as serpents and harmless as doves" (NKJV); "be wise as serpents and innocent as doves" (NRSV).[2]

Jesus also indicated the importance of acting wisely when He told the story of the "unjust steward" who was commended because he "had dealt shrewdly" (Luke 16:8) in taking action to secure a place for himself after his employment was terminated. Jesus concluded the parable by saying, "The sons of this world are more shrewd [KJV, "wiser"] in their generation than the sons of light." The implication is that Jesus' disciples can,

---

2. The word translated "wise" in Matthew 10:16 in the KJV is not the usual Greek word for "wisdom" (*sophos*), but *phronimos*. W. E. Vine says that the word means "prudent, sensible, practically wise." (W. E. Vine, "Wise, Wiser, Wisely," *An Expository Dictionary of New Testament Words* [Westwood, NJ: Fleming H. Revell Co., 1940, 1966], 222.) It is also found in Matt. 7:24 (the "wise man" who built his house on a rock); 24:45; 25:2, 4, 8, 9; Luke 12:42; 16:8; 1 Cor 10:15. Sellers Crain wrote, "The apostles were to exercise wisdom in their dealings with other men." (Sellers S. Crain, Jr., *Matthew 1-13, Truth for Today Commentary*, ed. Eddie Cloer [Searcy, Ark.: Resource Publications, 2010], 349.)

and should, learn something from the "sons of this world" about how to act wisely so that they can accomplish their righteous goals. Furthermore, Jesus Himself acted wisely (Mark 6:2), and at least implied His approval of wisdom when He said that the person who heard His words and did them was like "a wise man who built his house on the rock" (Matt 7:24), and when he told the parable about the five foolish and five wise virgins who "took their lamps and went out to meet the bridegroom" (Matt 25:1–13).

The epistles also recommend that Christians act wisely. Note the following passages:

- Christians should pray for a "spirit of wisdom" (Eph 1:17).
- James wrote, "If any of you lacks wisdom, let him ask of God, who gives to all liberally and without reproach, and it will be given to him" (Jam 1:5), and recommended that Christians practice what he called the "wisdom ... from above" (Jam 3:17, 18).
- Paul wrote, "Let your speech always be with grace, seasoned with salt, that you may know how you ought to answer each one" (Col 4:6). Or, as the CEV paraphrases: "Choose your words carefully ..."
- Paul recommended that Christians act wisely when he exhorted the Ephesians, "See then that you walk circumspectly, not as fools but as wise, redeeming the time, because the days are evil" (Eph 5:15, 16).
- Paul also said, "According to the grace of God which was given to me, as a wise master builder I have laid the foundation, and another builds on it. But let each one take heed how he builds on it" (1 Cor

- 3:10). Those who, like Paul, plant and build churches should do so wisely.

Perhaps the best passage from the epistles to demonstrate the importance of using wisdom in doing the work of the Lord is 1 Corinthians 9:19-22:

> For though I am free from all men, I have made myself a servant to all that I might win the more; and to the Jews I became as a Jew, that I might win Jews; to those who are under the law, as under the law, that I might win those who are under the law; to those who are without law, as without law (not being without law toward God, but under law toward Christ), that I might win those who are without law; to the weak I became as weak, that I might win the weak. I have become all things to all men, that I might by all means save some.

In his work Paul obviously used wisdom to accomplish the greatest amount of good.

Do these passages sound like God wants His children to blunder through life, giving no thought as to how they are to live their lives and influence others for Christ? Do they seem to say that a Christian should simply do what's right without concerning himself about how he does it? Or do they say that he should not only always do the right thing, but do it in the best way, the wisest way, the most effective way?

The New Testament not only requires Christians to act wisely, but it also contains numerous examples to illustrate how the apostles and evangelists in the first century sought to do their jobs in the most effective—thus, the wisest—way possible. In their preaching, for instance, they preached Christ to every audience, but they approached the subject differently based on the occasion and the hearers. Compare Peter's sermon on Pentecost (Acts 2), Philip's message to the Ethiopian eunuch (Acts 8), Peter's lesson to Cornelius (Acts 10), Paul's presentation in the synagogue at Antioch of Pisidia (Acts 13), and Paul's speech on Mars Hill in Athens (Acts 17). Every message points to Christ, but each begins differently. Why? Because the preachers used wisdom; they began in the way most likely to be effective with their particular audience. Again, Paul's missionary methods have been studied and used as a pattern for modern-day missions. Why? Because he went about the business of spreading the word in a very effective (very wise) way.

The same thing could be said about the way the epistles were written. These writers used words that were designed to elicit the responses they were seeking. One could, for example, almost use the book of Philemon as a short textbook on the art of rhetoric—on how to communicate persuasively. If someone objects, "But the people you are talking about were divinely inspired, and we are not," then they reinforce my argument. To speak and write persuasively—thus to act wisely—must be important because that's the way God inspired New Testament speakers and writers to communicate. So that must be the way He wants His Word to be communicated today. In other words, the New Testament gives ample evidence that the apostles and evangelists sought always to act wisely in their work for the Lord.

The examples above apply most obviously to those who preach and teach God's word, but they should not be limited to them. Every Christian is in the church-building business. We just have different roles to play. While the Christian carpenter builds houses, he also helps build the church by exercising a good influence in the community. Therefore, we can say that it is not just preachers who need to be "wise as serpents"—every Christian needs to do so. We all need to think carefully and act wisely because what we do—and whether we succeed—may have eternal consequences for someone.[3]

Limitations of Wisdom

As they attempt to put wisdom to work for themselves, Christians need to recognize its limitations. First, we need to understand that wisdom itself is morally neutral. The Old Testament provides examples of wisdom (as applied in persuasive speech) used for evil as well as for good.[4] Being wise, or smart, or highly educated, will not keep you from sinning. Solomon

---

3. One could also object that the New Testament speakers and writers who sought to communicate effectively (thus, wisely) did not always achieve their purpose. For instance, in Acts 7, Stephen spoke eloquently and persuasively, but all it got him was a martyr's death. We need to keep in mind that the results of our preaching/teaching are always dependent on the willingness of our hearers to believe and act upon the truth. Not everyone is good soil. The point is that we should always do the best we can to get the results we want (and that glorify God). To do so, we need to communicate as effectively as possible, recognizing that, even after we have done our best, some will still resist our message.

4. See, for example, the serpent's persuasive speech in Genesis 3:4, 5, and Rabshakeh's speech in 2 Kings 18:19–35.

was the wisest person on earth, but he sinned! Today a genius can use his great mental capacity either to bless mankind or to achieve evil purposes. Consequently, our encouragement to "act wisely" must always be accompanied by the admonition to "act righteously." A Christian must never use wisdom, or intelligence, to achieve unworthy or sinful objectives. Our use of wisdom must be limited by "the fear of the Lord" (Prov. 1:7).

Second, an individual's use of wisdom may also be limited by the fact that wisdom is relative. Some people are naturally wiser than others, and the application of wisdom may be limited by one's intelligence—and mental ability varies from one person to another.[5] Wisdom is sometimes an inborn trait, a gift that some have without having to work for it. Nevertheless, we can all become wiser if we strive to do so. We may never become as wise as Solomon (or those who are especially gifted with wisdom today), but we can learn to act more wisely in our daily lives.

A third limitation of wisdom is that those of us who try to use it are fallible human beings. Therefore, even though we want to act wisely, to do what is most effective, we often fall short. No one acts wisely all the time. We all suffer lapses in judgment. We make mistakes, sometimes because we speak or act before we think. We goof up, we err, we put our feet in our mouths. Nothing will guarantee that we will never make another mistake. All we can do is to guard our tongues, think before we act (or speak), and hope and pray that as we continue

---

5. It should also be noted that in our time "wisdom"—knowing how to apply knowledge, being able to deal effectively with people and problems—is not the same as either "(measured) intelligence" or "education." People can be smart and have a lot of "book learning," but be totally incompetent in solving practical problems.

to live we will grow wiser and wiser and generate fewer and fewer foul-ups. And God can, and will, sometimes providentially use our mistakes to bring glory to His name! As He has always done, He can bring good effects from bad causes. We may goof up and get fired—and that's bad. But then God may open the door for us to get a better job, where we can do more for Him—and that's good! So while we always ought to do our best to act wisely, we also need to be faithful to God and trust in Him to work "all things"—even our unwise errors—"together for good" (Rom. 8:28).

Wisdom in Our Lives

Even though the use of wisdom has these limitations, the Christian, knowing that the New Testament advises it, will strive to act wisely. That means that Christians will act in such a way—within the boundaries of what God permits—that they will most likely accomplish their objectives.

To that end, the Christian will: (1) Set goals that are definite and achievable. (2) Make plans to reach those goals. (3) Enlist the help he or she needs from others to achieve those goals. (4) Get the information needed—or the education required—to succeed at those goals. (5) Develop the talents needed to arrive at those goals. (6) Among those talents, he or she will cultivate the art of persuasive communication.[6] Christians will, of course, all along the way seek the help of the Lord, asking Him for wisdom (Jam 1:5) and utilizing the "wisdom that is from above" (Jam 3:17, 18). These requirements for success can be

---

6. Sometimes believers do these things naturally, but sometimes they need to be taught or encouraged to do them.

summed up in the words: Christians will act wisely! When Christians do so, they obey a biblical injunction. The result is likely to be a measure of success and prosperity that they would not have enjoyed if they had not acted wisely.

Conclusion

Finally, we must admit that sometimes the Christian way seems stupid—or, as Paul would say, "foolish" (1 Cor. 1:18)—rather than wise. If you can get ahead by cheating, does it make any sense (is it wise?) to not cheat? Do you think that onlookers thought Stephen was wise in his presentation of the gospel when it resulted in his death? Given the sinful world in which we live, how can we be both wise and righteous? There are two possible answers to that dilemma.

One is that if we are forced to choose between acting wisely—or doing what will bring success and prosperity in this life—and acting righteously, we must choose righteousness! Even if we appear to be stupid to others, we have to choose the right way, the "narrow gate" and the "narrow way" that leads to life (Matt 7:13, 14).

A second possible answer is that if we choose the narrow way, and refuse to sin, even if sinning would, in the short run, be more profitable, we are acting wisely! Wisdom leads to success, and the greatest success is not getting ahead in this life, but gaining eternal life! Living the Christian life requires us to live wisely—to live in such a way that we are likely to succeed, both in this life and that which is to come.

5

BECAUSE THEY HAVE HELP

Of this we can be sure. Life is going to hit us with difficult times—with tragedies, loss, sickness, disappointments. We will get sick. We will lose our job and maybe even get fired. Loved ones will die. We will be disappointed in love. Our teams will not always win. Our children won't always live up to expectations. Our great plans will come to naught. Our wonderful story or novel will be rejected. Our new house will require a $25,000 repair job. When such things happen, what do we do? Successful people cope. They somehow find a way to continue on with their life. They make the best of a bad thing, put their chin up, and go on living! People who can't overcome such problems are likely neither to succeed nor to prosper.

The point of this chapter is simple: Christians are likely to succeed in life because they have available to them a number of resources which enable them to cope with the difficulties they encounter. Therefore, they are likely to overcome their problems—and so to prosper. The Christian's ability to deal successfully with stress has been noticed by those who study happiness. One article reported,

> Religious service attendance promotes social interaction and friendship with others, and Gallup analyses have clearly shown that time spent socially and social

networks themselves are positively associated with high wellbeing. Religion generally involves more meditative states and faith in a higher power, both of which have been widely used as methods to lower stress, reduce depression, and promote happiness. Religion provides mechanisms for coping with setbacks and life's problems, which in turn may reduce stress, worry, and anger. Many religions, including Christianity, by far the dominant religion in the U.S., embody tenets of positive relationships with one's neighbors and charitable acts, which may lead to a more positive mental outlook.[1]

In this chapter I want to do three things: (1) make it plain that Christians will have problems, (2) affirm that God has provided them with all the resources they need to deal with those problems, and (3) present the means by which they can access those resources.

Christians Will Have Problems

Before we discuss how Christians can overcome their problems, we need to make the point that—contrary to the beliefs of the health and wealth gospel—Christians will experience difficulties. God did not promise an easy life for faithful Christians. Jesus was a "man of sorrows" and just as He bore His cross, Christians must be willing to bear their crosses (Matt

---

1. Frank Newport, Dan Witters, and Sangeeta Agrawal, "Religious Americans Enjoy Higher Wellbeing," https://news.gallup.com/poll/152723/religious-americans-enjoy-higher-wellbeing.aspx.

16:24). Paul had a thorn in the flesh and was persecuted almost everywhere he went; all but one of the apostles died as martyrs; the godly are promised persecution (1 Tim 3:12; Matt 5:10–12). Even faithful Christians get sick and die (Acts 9:36, 37). If God does not keep Christians from having problems, how are they better off than others? They have help others do not have.

The Christian's Sources Of Help

When Christians face problems, where can they go for help? Many cities provide resources to assist their inhabitants, but Christians have resources which are not available to others.

Heavenly help is available. God is always present to bless His people (Heb 13:5). Jesus Christ the Son of God is with us (Matt 28:20; Eph 3:17; Col 1:27). The Holy Spirit has been given to Christians (Acts 2:38; 5:32; Gal 4:6) and He strengthens them (Eph 3:16). Angels are "ministering spirits" sent to serve the people of God (Heb 1:14). Heaven—the Father, the Son, the Holy Spirit; and even the angels—is prepared to help us in our struggles!

Fellow Christians in the body of Christ are a valuable resource when we need help. God intended for Christ's church to be composed of congregations of believers, whose corporate task would not only be to worship God and spread His word, but also to encourage and edify members of the church. Consequently, Christians are often told to help one another. The New Testament says that we are to:

- "love one another" (John 13:34, 35; 15:17; 1 John 4:7);
- "bear one another's burdens" (Gal 6:2);

- "be devoted to one another" (Rom 12:10, NASB);
- build one another up (Rom 14:19);
- "encourage one another" (Heb 3:13, NASB; 10:24; 1 Thess 5:11);
- assemble with one another (Heb 10:25);
- teach and admonish one another as we sing to one another (Col 3:16);
- "be patient" with one another (1 Thess 5:14);
- confess our sins to one another (Jam 5:16);
- "pray for one another" (Jam 5:16);
- "be hospitable to one another" (1 Pet 4:9);
- serve one another (1 Pet 4:10).

In the early church their love for one another caused Christians to freely give up what they owned to share with their brothers and sisters in need (Acts 2:44, 45; 4:32–37; see also Acts 11:28–30; Rom. 15:25–27; 2 Cor 8, 9).

To cope with the difficulties of life everyone needs a support system. Christians have a built-in support system. They are "members of one another" (Rom 12:5). For the Christian in trouble, this fact means that in his local congregation he has access to a wonderful reservoir of assistance.

So if there is a death in the family, a sudden and unexpected tragedy, if sickness or a debilitating disease strikes, etc., as a rule, Christians rush to help their brother or sister in trouble—with food and shelter and clothing and helping hands and tender sympathy and loving words. And, just as in New Testament times, Christians are willing to open their pocketbooks (and checkbooks) to assist fellow Christians in financial trouble. Consequently Christians who have problems have not only divine assistance, but human help in overcoming those problems. That makes them better able to cope, and more likely to succeed in the long run.

Help from Biblical Promises

Biblical promises, properly understood and applied, can enable the Christian to overcome problems. God's word is valuable (Psa 119; 19:10); it is able to "build [us] up" and give us an "inheritance among all those who are sanctified" (Acts 20:32). It contains "great and precious promises" (2 Pet 1:4) which empower us to live the Christian life. What are some of the promises God's word makes to us?

Anxiety has always been a problem. People worry about many things, but especially about whether or not they will be able to survive from day to day. The Christian has the advantage of being promised that God will supply his needs. Jesus said to His disciples, "Do not be worried about your life, as to what you will eat or what you will drink, nor for your body, as to what you will put on ... but seek first [God's] kingdom and His righteousness, and all these things will be added to you" (Matt 6:25, 33, NASB; see also Phil 4:6). The Bible promises that God knows what we need, and He will supply it.[2] Therefore, we need not be worried or anxious.

We may fear the future, fear the possibility of failure, fear being found out, fear the consequences of past mistakes, fear the likelihood that we will lose what we have. Jesus quiets our fears, just as He did the fears of his disciples, by saying, "Peace I leave with you; My peace I give to you; not as the world gives

---

2. It should be noted that Jesus does not here promise to give us everything we want; He promises us what we need, and God's definition of what we need may differ from our own.

do I give to you. Let not your heart be troubled, neither let it be afraid" (John 14:27b; see also Matt 14:27; Mark 6:50; 1 John 4:18). We can overcome our fears if we will cast "all [our] anxiety on Him because He cares for [us]" (1 Pet 5:7, NASB). When we do, we will know what Paul calls "the peace of God, which surpasses all understanding" (Phil 4:7). Christians are promised peace to replace their fears and anxiety.

At one time or another, we all feel that we have been mistreated or persecuted. What do we do then? Retaliate? Have a fit? Retreat and pout? Become bitter and angry? Let our resentment turn into hatred and let it simmer, maybe for months or years? Perhaps the most difficult command for Christians to obey is: "Love your enemies, bless those who curse you, do good to those who hate you, and pray for those who spitefully use you and persecute you" (Matt 5:44). The Bible calls on Christians to love and forgive and do good to those who have done them wrong (see Jesus' example in Luke 23:34; see also Rom 12:19–21).

How can anyone do that? The answer? Only with God's help! Patience—which would include the ability to treat your enemies with love—is part of the fruit the Holy Spirit bears in the Christian's life (Gal 5:22); Paul prayed that the Colossians might be "strengthened with all power, according to His glorious might, for the attainment of all steadfastness and patience" (Col 1:11, NASB).

With God's help, we can do what would otherwise be impossible! We can forgive our enemies! And when we do, we relieve ourselves of the need to bear a grudge and harbor hatred in our hearts. We consequently open ourselves to the entrance of joy and contentment—and make our own success more likely.

We didn't get the job we wanted, or we didn't pass the test, or we didn't make the team, or we didn't get accepted at the school of our choice, or we failed at work. Consequently we are disappointed; we get discouraged; we feel depressed; we are ready to quit. How does the Bible help when we are down? It brings good news! Even if no one else loves us, God does (John 3:16), and Jesus does (John 13:34)! We don't have to succeed in this life to succeed in another. All we have to do is be "faithful until death" and we will receive our crown of triumph (Rev 2:10).

Furthermore, failure doesn't need to be final. Perseverance pays off. Christians share Paul's conviction: "I can do all things through Christ who strengthens me" (Phil 4:13). We understand "all things" to involve the modifier "within His will;" but Christians can, in His strength, when they have failed, pick themselves up and try again, believing in God's ability to accomplish great things through them. We can accomplish our objectives because God is on our side!

Everyone experiences losses in this life. Our goods may be stolen, our house may burn down, the stock market may crash, or we might lose our job or means of support. When we lose much, or everything, what do we do then? Christians have an advantage over materialists in dealing with such losses. They know that they cannot lose everything. If all material possessions disappear, they still have spiritual blessings—God as Father, Christ as Savior, the Holy Spirit as strengthener, the angels as helpers, heaven as hope. They have laid up "treasures in heaven, where neither moth nor rust destroys and where thieves do not break in and steal" (Matt 6:20).

Whatever happens, the Christian can take comfort from the promise that the Lord will never forsake him or her. Nothing in this world can separate us from Christ and the blessings He provides. Paul put it well:

> If God is for us, who can be against us? ... Who shall separate us from the love of Christ? Shall tribulation, or distress, or persecution, or famine, or nakedness, or peril, or sword? ... In all these things we are more than conquerors through Him who loved us. For I am persuaded that neither death nor life, nor angels nor principalities nor powers, nor things present nor things to come, nor height nor depth, nor any other created thing, shall be able to separate us from the love of God which is in Christ Jesus our Lord. (Rom 8:31, 35, 37-39)

With such a promise, nothing in the world—no loss, no defeat, no problem—should overthrow the Christian's conviction that he or she will, in spite of everything, be all right.

Christians (like everyone else) struggle to understand "Why?" Why do children die? Why do the innocent suffer? Why don't I ever get any breaks? Why does success elude me? When people try to answer those questions, everyone (including unbelievers) want to believe that "everything happens for a purpose." But only Christians have the assurance found in Romans 8:28: "And we know that all things work together for good to those who love God, to those who are the called according to His purpose."

Christians are promised that God is still at work in the world today—not miraculously, but providentially. Therefore, they can believe that "all things"—good things and bad things—are being worked together "for good"—not necessarily for a pleasant life, but for "good," as defined by God, for ultimate good—for the Christian's sake. The non-Christian may hope the same thing is true in his or her circumstances, but God has given no assurance of that fact.

We may not see the "good" immediately—we may be unable to see the meaning or the purpose behind the tragedies of life, but we may understand it eventually, years later. We may then say, "What happened was terrible, but it resulted in this good thing happening." Believing in the providence of God and in the promise of Romans 8:28, the Christian can survive, and thrive, even when circumstances are dangerous or difficult, and life turns bitter and black.

Almost everyone experiences the feeling of guilt.[3] That feeling can overwhelm people and leave them incapable of constructive action. Even if it does not, guilt can negatively affect a person's life. Many of an individual's problems are really the outgrowth of his or her feelings of guilt. The Christian way is uniquely equipped to help one overcome feelings of guilt. It provides forgiveness of sins! Jesus came and died that we might be forgiven! All we have to do is to turn to Him in faith and to obey His requirements (Acts 2:38), and we will have the forgiveness of our sins! Christians then can be grateful for the constant daily cleansing of the blood of Christ (1 John 1:7).

Having had the burden of guilt lifted from their shoulders, Christians can rejoice and live a life of love, untroubled by the weight of their past sins. They can face life with calm confidence; and when they do, they are likely to be able to cope with

---

3. Guilt is universal; all sin (Rom 3:23) and so become guilty before God. The *feeling* of guilt should also be universal, but unfortunately it is not. Some people can and do break laws and hurt others without ever feeling guilt.

their problems and succeed at their jobs.

Perhaps our greatest fear is death. Paul called "death" the "last enemy" (1 Cor 15:26). How can we cope with that fear? For the faithful Christian, death loses much of its terror, since it is the doorway to a brighter future. Paul, when he was faced with the possibility of martyrdom, even said, "For to me, to live is Christ and *to die is gain* ... to depart and be with Christ ... is far better" (Phil 1:21, 23). Why "better"? Because heaven will be a place of unsurpassed beauty and unparalleled grandeur. More important, it will be a place where God will be in the midst of His people, and He "will wipe away every tear from their eyes; and there shall be no more death, nor sorrow, nor crying; and there shall be no more pain" (Rev 21:4). And most important: Heaven will be forever! There will be no end to the joyous life we experience there! Thus, Christians can endure—they can cope with—the tragedies of this life because they know that they will one day experience a better life—forever!

That fact becomes especially meaningful as a person grows older. When we get old, we are likely to lose our health, lose our mobility, lose our sight and/or our hearing, lose (or have drastically reduced) our income, lose the respect we once had from others, lose our sense of dignity and worth. In their old age Christians can rejoice in the fact that, though we are farther from our youthful triumphs, we are nearer home! Even more than other disciples we can believe what we sing: "Earth holds no treasures but perish with using, However precious they be; Yet there's a country to which I am going. Heaven holds all to me."[4] To the non-Christian, advanced old age may be be nothing but a time of unrelenting darkness and despair; to the faithful Christian, it is a prelude to glory.

---

4. "Earth Holds No Treasures," words by Tillit S. Teddlie.

How Christians Can Access The Help God Provides

How can the Christian access these resources? How can we take advantage of all the provisions God has made so that we can find happiness and success in spite of life's trials? God has made available to us wonderful blessings that will help us in times of trouble. How do we receive the benefits of those blessings? We need to do four things:

First, to receive help from God we need to ask for it. We need to pray. Prayer gives Christians access to divine help. Jesus promised that our prayers would be answered (Matt 7:7-11, see also 1 John 5:14). In New Testament times, when Christians were troubled, they prayed (see, for example, Acts 4:23-31; 12:12).

Too often, when faced with problems and needing relief, Christians are like the disciples of whom James spoke: "You do not have because you do not ask" (Jam 4:2b). We need the faith of the Psalmist who wrote, "I will lift up my eyes to the mountains—from whence comes my help? My help comes from the Lord, Who made heaven and earth" (Psa 121:1, 2). We need to pray frequently and fervently, believing that we will receive what we ask for, but always saying, "Your will be done." We need to trust that God will in fact answer our prayers in a way that coincides with His plans.

Second, to have access to God's resources, we need to associate with other disciples. In other words, to receive the benefits of being members of the body of Christ, we have to act like members of that body—by assembling regularly with the saints, for instance (Heb 10:25). Interestingly, those who do research on the relationship between happiness and religion find that the act of attending church regularly contributes to a person's wellbeing.

Why? Because people need other people. God made us social beings, and, for our health's sake, we need to have social relationships. When we are connected solidly with other members of the church, we will likely be better able to cope with stress; we will probably have better mental health; and we will usually be more successful.

Third, to take advantage of God's blessings, we need to read, study, meditate on, and believe God's word. The Bible contains the wonderful promises we have described. But you will never benefit from those promises if you do not know about them. Christians need to read God's word daily, study it, memorize it, think about it, believe it, and meditate on it. God's word needs to become so much a part of the Christian's life that when a problem arises, meaningful scriptures will come to mind automatically. For example, when bad things happen, we should immediately think, "All things work together for good …" or, "Cast all your cares on Him, for He cares for you …" Believing what God has said and meditating on His word—thinking about what it means—can help us cope with both the ordinary and extraordinary stresses of life.

Fourth, we need to live as God's word directs. Just knowing the Bible or believing the Bible will not help much unless you put into practice what you know and believe. Sometimes the only solution to difficult circumstances is simply to grit your teeth and "do the right thing." If we keep acting like Christians—no matter what we feel like doing—we may be surprised at how acting right helps solve our problems and, in the end, leaves us feeling better.

Such is especially true of the biblical admonition to return good for evil. The way of the world is to hurt the one who hurt you, to get revenge, to bear a grudge. These reactions are never best for the person wronged. Rather, it is always best to forgive and do good! When we do, we will more likely find peace of mind. Stress will disappear, and we can resume our journey on the way to success.

Conclusion

Christians are fortunate in that they have resources to deal with problems. In fact, Christians have an amazing ability to recover from setbacks. One of the people I interviewed for this study said, "I call it resilience. The Christian culture is a resilient culture. It can go backwards if necessary—if circumstances warrant—in order later to resume its forward movement. Modern culture, in general, is not like that."[5]

God provides the resources the Christian needs to overcome life's trials. Because of the help of God, the help of other disciples, and the promises found in God's word, Christians who pray, associate with other Christians, read and believe and meditate on the Bible, and constantly try to obey it, can overcome their problems. They can live a life of constant joy (Phil 4:4), unworried by past defeats, undeterred by present foes, and unafraid of what the future holds. Experiencing peace within, they can give their attention to the challenge of their jobs—with the result that they are more likely to succeed than they would if they could not cope with the problems of life.

There's a "catch" of course. What we have said *can* be true of Christians, but is not necessarily the case. Why? Because the

---

5. Ian Shepherd, in an interview with Coy Roper, conducted in Abilene, Texas, on December 10, 2015..

appropriation of the available blessings depends on faith—and Christians, being human, often fail to believe in, or understand, or appreciate, or accept, the blessings that go with being a child of God. So if Christians cannot cope with life's difficulties, it's not because they lack the tools to succeed; it's because they fail to use the tools that God has placed at their disposal.

6

BECAUSE THEY ARE GOOD STEWARDS

One reason Christians are likely to prosper in this life is that they practice good stewardship. A successful Christian entrepreneur attributed his success, in part, to the fact that he practiced good stewardship principles. He said, "I got my ideas about stewardship from the Bible, from church and from Bible classes. Stewardship was engrained in me because it was a biblical concept."[1]

The principle of stewardship is illustrated by the parable of the talents found in Matthew 25:14–30. Jesus told about a man who went on a long journey and "entrusted his possessions" to three of his servants. He gave five "talents"[2] to one, two to

---

1. Kevin Batten, from an interview conducted by Coy Roper on November 20, 2015, in Abilene, Texas. Kevin cited the parable of the talents in Matthew 25 to illustrate the meaning of stewardship. He pointed out that in the parable stewardship involved taking a risk, and suggested that the practice of stewardship today involves taking risks. In a sense, whatever steps we take to improve ourselves or to help others are risky endeavors because they involve the possibility of failure. Nevertheless, the parable suggests that we ought to take such risks (rather than following the lead of the man who buried his talent and therefore took no risk) if we are to be good stewards.

2. A "talent" was a sum of money. A footnote in *The New Oxford Annotated Bible* says, "A talent was more than fifteen years' wages of a laborer."

another, and one to the third. Two of the servants used their money to make more money; the one who had only one talent "dug in the ground and hid his lord's money."

When the master returned "after a long time," the servant who had been given five talents had gained five more, and so returned ten to his master; the one who had received two had gained two more, and gave back four. The master was pleased with both and said to them, "Well done ... enter into the joy of your lord." However, the servant who had only received one talent simply gave it back to the master, saying, "I knew you to be a hard man, reaping where you have not sown, and gathering where you have not scattered seed. And I was afraid, and went and hid your talent in the ground. Look, there you have what is yours" (v. 24, 25). The master responded to him by taking away the talent and giving it to the servant who already had ten talents, by calling him a "wicked and lazy servant" and an "unprofitable servant," and by having him cast out "into the outer darkness."

The idea of stewardship is thus based on four great truths:

- Everything belongs to God.
- God entrusts men with "talents"—that is, He gives them whatever they have, including material and immaterial blessings. Even though we have possession of these things, they still belong to God.
- God expects us to use what He has given us in His service, for His benefit, to His glory.
- God will one day call everyone to account for how they have used what He has placed at their disposal.

Since Christians believe in this principle, they take seriously the need to make good use of everything God has blessed them with. The result is that their "talents" (that is, the blessings they have received from God) are likely to be multiplied. Consider the application of the practice of stewardship in several areas.

The Stewardship of Our Bodies

We are stewards of our physical bodies. Our bodies are not our own; we were "bought with a price" (1 Cor 6:19, 20). That fact means, for one thing, that we are not free to abuse or misuse our bodies as we see fit. We are not our own; therefore we need to treat the body as if it were the "temple of the Holy Spirit," because it is!

For another, since our bodies belong to the Lord, we will do our best to take care of them. We will want to eat the right foods, exercise, get enough rest, etc. Our goal should be to keep our bodies as healthy as possible for as long as possible so that we can use them to do God's work as many years as possible.

The Stewardship of Our Minds

We are also stewards of our minds, of our ability to learn, to remember, to think, to reason. People have differing levels of mental ability just as they differ physically. Some have bodies that are taller and stronger; some have minds that are more capable of certain kinds of learning. Whatever our mental ability—whether we are like the five-talent servant, the two-talent servant, or the one-talent servant—we need to dedicate it to God's use, to accomplish His purposes. To do so will require that, as a rule, Christians get as much formal education or training as they need, so they can be good stewards of the mind God entrusted him with.

The Stewardship of Our Talents

Christians are also stewards of the talents, or abilities, God has given them. People have different talents. Some are good at figuring things out or remembering facts; some are good at working with their hands; some are good at dealing with people; some are strong; some are fast; some are musically gifted; some are talented artists; some are good speakers; some are gifted at cooking; some are great at encouraging other people. But everyone has one or more talents he or she was born with—one or more talents given to him or her by God.

What should the Christian do with the talents he or she has? We aren't left to wonder. God has answered that question in the New Testament. There He calls those talents "gifts." He says that all members of the body have been given gifts, and that we should use those gifts to build up the body, (see 1 Cor 12; Rom 12; 1 Pet 4:10, 11).[3] In other words, we should use them in His service.

I conclude, therefore, that we are stewards of our talents. What does that require? To be good stewards of our talents we must:

(1) Discover our talents.

---

3. The "gifts" referred to in the New Testament are sometimes, or usually, miraculous gifts of the Holy Spirit which were given by the laying on of the apostles' hands. These miraculous gifts are no longer available to Christians today. But the principles related to their use apply to the non-miraculous gifts God blesses His people with today.

(2) Develop our talents. Do whatever is necessary to make the most of our God-given abilities.

(3) Dedicate our talents to the cause of Christ. To do so might mean that we would choose a "Christian vocation" (become a preacher or missionary, for instance), but it would not necessarily require us to do so. We can be a Christian mechanic, or professor, or musician, or actor, or writer, or lawyer, etc., and dedicate ourselves and our occupation to helping others and glorifying God.

It may be tempting to slide through life without thought for where we are going or what we are doing or what we might be able to do if we tried. But Christians are not likely to choose that alternative. They will deliberately set out to use those talents in the best way possible. To do so is a formula for success. People who successfully use their talents usually prosper.

The Stewardship of Our Time

God has not only given us our talents, but He has also given us our time. By that I mean that time—the twenty-four hours a day at our disposal—is a precious commodity and a gift of God. Since God has given us our time, He expects us to be good stewards of that time, especially by using it in a way that will be profitable to His cause.

Perhaps the biggest problem of many of us is that we waste too much time. We know that there are many things we could do that would be good for ourselves, for others, and for Christ's cause; but instead of using our time for good, we fritter it away on useless pursuits. We are more likely to waste time than anything else.

To say that we need to use our time wisely and well (see Eph 5:16) is not to say that we should never take any time for rest and relaxation. It is rather to say that we should be conscious of how much time we use on activities that are of no value to anyone. It is to say that we should not spend too much time on worthless pursuits.

If we were to make good use of our time, we might be surprised at what we could accomplish—at how much we could learn, at the number of books we could read (or how much we could learn about the Bible), at how many encouraging letters we could write or visits we could make, at the way we could enhance our formal education, etc. Almost certainly, one thing that helps people succeed is that they use their time well.

Stewardship of Our Opportunities

We are also stewards of our opportunities, in that we should see the opportunities that come to us as given by God to provide us with the chance to bring glory to His name. In the parable in Matthew 25 the master gave the servants money, but he also gave them the opportunity to use their money for his benefit. God gives us talents (gifts, abilities), and then He gives us opportunities to use those talents in His service.

The idea is that God closes doors and opens doors.[4] When a "door" is opened, the Christian needs to ask himself or herself: "Is God making this opportunity available to me because He

---

4. Paul uses this metaphor in 1 Corinthians 16:9: "For a wide door for effective service has opened to me, and there are many adversaries" (NASB).

wants me to serve in this way in this place at this time?" Sometimes it is hard to answer that question, but the Christian needs to be open to the possibility that the One who opens a door is the Lord Himself.

For example, my first fulltime preaching job was with a congregation in a small town in Texas. In 1959, my wife and I (we had only been married a little over a year), for various reasons, decided we wanted to find another place to preach. I wrote one or two congregations which needed preachers, but before I heard from them I got a call out of the blue asking if I would be interested in teaching at Western Christian College in Weyburn, Saskatchewan, Canada.[5] We thought about it for a week, and then accepted the job. Interestingly, one reason we were looking for another job was that we felt we were about to starve to death; but we agreed to go to Canada and teach for about $1,600 less per year than we were being paid at the time (and in 1959 $1,600 a year was quite a bit of money to us). Why would we do such a thing? I'm not sure, but I think that at the time I saw that opportunity as coming from God. Subsequent events have not changed my mind. To say the least, if we had declined that opportunity, our life would have been very different. Some things we have done probably would not have been accomplished.

So before you say "No" to an opportunity, ask yourself: Did it come from God? Is He providing me with a unique opportunity to serve Him? If the answer is "Yes," the principle of stewardship would suggest that you should walk through that open door and see what God has in store for you on the other side. Perhaps by this means God is propelling you into a

---

5. Western Christian College was basically a Christian high school, serving grades 9-12, with some "Grade 13" (college) students.

different field where you will find success, for yourself and, more important, for His cause.

The Stewardship of Our Possessions

Frequently the discussion of stewardship is limited to the discussion of the Christian's use of money—and maybe even limited to the subject of the Christian's responsibility to give his or her money to the Lord. From what has been said, I hope that you can see that the principle of stewardship applies, not just to money or to our giving, but to the whole of our lives. Nevertheless, it does apply to our money.

Whatever we have—our money and all our possessions—comes from God. We have control of it; in a sense we "own" it because we can decide what we will do with it (Acts 5:4). But we are responsible to use it in a way that pleases God and brings glory to His name. Someday God will call us to account for how we have used the earthly goods He has placed at our disposal. Since we are stewards of our money (and the possessions that money can buy), how should we use it? Two points need to be made.

First, we should use our money wisely. Glen McMillan, who has presented lessons on stewardship to numerous congregations, told me, "As I did more presentations, I realized the bigger challenge was to convince people that either one controlled money or it controlled you."[6] To make sure that we control our money rather than letting it control us, we need to use it wisely. The fact that we are to be good stewards of our

---

6. Glen McMillan, email to Coy Roper, December 23, 2015. Glen owned an automobile dealership in Kennedy, Saskatchewan, Canada before he retired.

money should influence all our purchasing decisions. What car should we buy? Do I really need a new set of golf clubs? Is this house a good investment? How much money should we spend on our vacation? The point is that, as stewards of our money, we will think about such questions before we make impulsive decisions. Wisdom also suggests that we need to avoid unnecessary debt. We also ought to save and/or invest some of what we have now to help meet needs we may have in the future. Obviously, if we are careful about how we spend our money, and exercise wisdom by saving and investing some of it, we are more likely to prosper than we would if we gave no thought to the subject. People who have an "easy come, easy go" attitude with regard to their income and outgo are not likely to do well financially.

Second, we should use our money generously. God did not intend for us to be selfish with the money and possessions He put into our care. We are commanded to work so that we will be able to give to those who are in need (Eph 4:28). Therefore, Christians who practice stewardship are generous to others, both with their money and with the possessions that they have purchased with their money. One wealthy Christian businessperson I interviewed for this book put it well. He said, "It bugs me to see some brothers who have a lot of money who are stingy with it, who are legendary for being cheap. I want to ask them: Is that the way you would treat the Lord? Are you being generous, or tight, with the Lord? If we are not as generous with people as we would be with the Lord, then I think our soul is in jeopardy."[7]

---

7. Bruce Davis, in an interview with Coy Roper, conducted on December 18, 2015, in Abilene, Texas.

Christians are to give to those who are in need (Gal 6:10; Jam 1:27; Acts 2, 4, 5; Matt 25:31–46). And they should use what they own to benefit others. What is your house for? To live in, yes. But in addition, maybe God let you have that house to use to show hospitality to others. Maybe God gave you your car to use it to take people to church services or to doctors' appointments.

In addition, we should give part of our money to the Lord. How much? Although the Law of Moses required ten percent, the New Testament does not specify a certain amount or percentage that Christians should give. It does say that we should give as we have been prospered (1 Cor 16:1, 2). We should also give liberally (2 Cor 8:2) and cheerfully (2 Cor 9:7). Will being generous cause us to be blessed? Will sharing our goods, with others and with God, result in God's giving us greater prosperity? Yes, the New Testament teaches that if we give generously we will be blessed (2 Cor 9:8–11), but not necessarily (as the health and wealth hucksters claim) with more money. The blessings we receive from giving generously, like all the blessings we receive from obeying Christ, are spiritual in nature. If we obey our Lord, we are promised spiritual blessings in this life, and an eternal home hereafter. Nevertheless, it seems to me that it is possible that giving generously will help one succeed and prosper even in this life. Why? Because a person who gives generously to the Lord is likely to develop a generous personality. One who gives liberally to others becomes a more loving, giving, outgoing person, who is genuinely interested in meeting the needs of others.[8] Because of this, doors of opportunity are likely to be opened. Having a generous spirit may then make possible more opportunities to prosper.

If such is true, the prosperity of the liberal person is not the result of a biblical guarantee, or of the promises of the prosperity gospel. It is rather the consequence of the way that God made the universe and the way that He created humankind. When nothing evil gets in the way, generous people are more likely to succeed than miserly individuals.[9] Even if the giving of our money does not result in our financial success, the Bible still gives this assurance: "It is more blessed to give than to receive" (Acts 20:35). We have Christ's assurance that our giving will bless, not just those who receive our gifts, but us.

Conclusion

How could we sum up the principle of stewardship as it applies to the Christian? One should conclude that since we are but

---

8. This statement reverses the order we usually accept. We generally believe that generous people give generously. We are saying here that those who give generously become generous people. The feeling or attitude or personality trait follows the conscious act. When we consciously and deliberately (and habitually) give, regardless of how we "feel" about giving, we become better people, more giving people. The idea that the correct attitude follows the correct act is implied by Jesus' words, "Where your treasure is, there your heart will be also" (Matt 6:21).

9. Several of the people I interviewed for this book testified that they felt that because they had given generously to the Lord, they had been liberally blessed by Him. I would not say that this proves the truth of the prosperity gospel, but it does suggest that those who give liberally are likely to be blessed, even materially—perhaps for the reason just discussed. At any rate, whatever the reason, Christians should thank God for their blessings, whether spiritual or material.

stewards of our bodies, our minds, our talents, our time, our opportunities, and our money or possessions—that none of these things really belongs to us but they all belong to God. We should consider ourselves stewards of our lives. In other words, "you are not your own ...you were bought with a price" (1 Cor 6:19, 20). You have been "redeemed [bought back]," not "with corruptible things, like silver or gold ... but with the precious blood of Christ" (1 Pet 1:18, 19). Therefore, like Paul, you have been "crucified with Christ;" it is no longer you "who live, but Christ lives in [you]" (Gal 2:20). Consequently, as a Christian your primary task on earth is to "present your bod[y] [and everything you are and have] a living sacrifice, holy, acceptable to God" (Rom 12:1). In other words, we should consider ourselves stewards of our lives in their entirety. Everything we are and have belongs to God, and we should use it all to His glory. Loving God with all our heart, soul, mind, and strength (Mark 12:30) leaves nothing for ourselves. All is to be given to God.

If you give yourself completely to the Lord, then all else will follow. It will only be natural and right for you to dedicate your body, your mind, your abilities, your time, your opportunities, and your money to God. You will rejoice in the privilege of serving God with all of your life. If you have this one aim in life—to please God and do His will (see Phil 3:13, 14)—you are more likely to succeed in every way. And success usually means, not necessarily riches or wealth, but greater material prosperity.

CONCLUSION TO PART 1

If Christians follow Christ's instructions they will be more likely to succeed—even in non-religious matters—than if they don't ... and we assume that success in the secular world will usually be rewarded with greater financial prosperity. Therefore, I have concluded that Christians are likely to prosper materially. I have defined that prosperity to be relative to one's own abilities and to the prosperity of others in their group. And we have said that this principle will generally be true in times and places where Christians are not discriminated against. (It will also be true for people who are not Christians but who do the things that Christians are told to do in the Bible.)

We have asserted that Christians are likely to succeed and prosper because they, in obedience to biblical requirements, are people who . . .

- Work hard for a living,
- Obey the law,
- Practice Christian virtues,
- Act wisely,
- Take advantage of the resources available to Christians,
- And practice good stewardship.

If they do these things Christians are far more likely to succeed in this life than they would if they did not obey these requirements. Who would disagree with this proposition?

In an interview, Dusty Rhodes, a successful trial lawyer, testified to the practical value of Christianity. He said,

> My practice of Christianity, along with God's leading, has been very meaningful to me. It has helped me greatly in what I have done with my life. I give God the credit for everything I have accomplished. The legal profession requires excellence if you are going to succeed. As a trial lawyer, I approached my job with a basic Christian

viewpoint that God will oversee the process so that right will generally win out in the end. Being a Christian, I had to understand and distinguish right from wrong. You have to adopt a view of right and wrong and stay with it. In the legal system you have to make it clear that there can be no violation of your own sense of ethics. And all the things that Christians are supposed to do should be included in the excellence that a lawyer strives for. In fact, I would say that it would give anyone an upper hand if [they] realized and practiced these things.[10]

The point is that living like a Christian will help you succeed, whatever your occupation. Whether you are in the retail business, or the legal business, or the farming business, or the education business, or any other business, following Christ's directions will indeed give you the "upper hand." Besides that, there is this good news. When Christians falter and fail—as we all do sometimes—to live up to Christ's standards, we are promised forgiveness (1 John 1:7–9). As long as we live, failure need never be final. And the best news is that, for Christians, whether they prosper in this life or not, there is the promise of eternity in heaven. There we will certainly prosper. We will receive a "crown of life" (Rev 2:10).

What should all this mean to us? In our society, in this time and place, being a follower of Christ does not deprive us of anything worthwhile. Indeed, being a faithful disciple is likely to make our lives on earth better, more productive, happier. We are likely to live longer, enjoy life more, and experience greater prosperity than if we were not Christians. That fact should not make us smug or proud. Rather, we should be humbly grateful.

10. Dusty Rhodes, in an interview conducted by Coy Roper in Abilene, Texas, December 13, 2015.

Isn't it wonderful that God loved us enough that He not only blesses us with spiritual life here and eternal life hereafter, but with an abundant life on this earth? Furthermore, that fact just might be interesting to people who are not yet Christians. Why choose Christ? Because you are lost and need to be forgiven in order to escape eternal punishment and enjoy an eternal reward. At the same time, maybe a non-Christian considering whether to accept the Lord would be interested in knowing that becoming a child of God will not put him or her at a disadvantage in this life. In fact, it might help to realize that following Jesus is rewarding, not only in eternity, but also in this life.

However, to say that Christians generally prosper is not altogether satisfying to many disciples. We know of many children of God who haven't prospered, who instead have suffered, sometimes even because they are Christians. Frequently Christians themselves feel cheated because they don't see themselves as prospering. That's the discussion in the second part of this book: "And Why They Don't."

PART 2

AND WHY THEY DON'T

When I told my Christian family and friends that I was going to write a book on "why Christians prosper," many of them reacted negatively. As far as they were concerned, Christians, as a rule, in this day and time, do *not* prosper—or at least not to the extent that they should. Several of them would have been glad to use themselves as exhibit A to disprove my thesis. Their thoughts went something like this:

> "I have been faithful to Christ. I have tried hard to do His will, but I have been disappointed so many times. And now I know of so many others—people who are not Christians, sinful and evil people, sometimes even people who don't have half my intelligence or education or ability—and yet they have a lot more than I have! How can you say that Christians are likely to prosper in the face of my experience?"

Their feelings are understandable. If Christians can prosper, and should prosper, why don't they? It might be well, before I begin to try to answer that question, to note that God's people have been asking it from earliest times. That's what the book of Job is about: Job was a righteous man who prospered—and then it was all taken from him. Why?

With the giving of the Law of Moses, the question became even more acute. Numerous passages in the Old Testament seem to promise prosperity to the individual Israelite if he would just be faithful to God. God promised Israel that if they would obey His commandments, He would "give [them] rain in its season" so that the land would "yield its produce" (Lev. 26:4). The Psalmist said, "Blessed is the man who walks not in the counsel of the ungodly ... his delight is in the law of the Lord ... whatever he does shall prosper" (Psa 1:1-3). In Proverbs we read, "Trust in the Lord with all your heart ... honor the Lord with your possessions . . . so your barns will be filled with plenty" (Prov 3:5, 9, 10).

Yet even in Old Testament times God's saints were often disappointed because they were not favored with success. Job was not the only righteous person who had reason to complain about what he saw as God's unfair treatment. The writer of Psalm 73 said, "I was envious of the boastful, when I saw the prosperity of the wicked" (Psalm 73:3). Habakkuk asked God, "Why do You look on those who deal treacherously, and hold your tongue when the wicked devours one more righteous than he?" (Hab 1:13b).

So the question we are dealing with in the next several chapters is not new. God's people have been asking it from earliest days: Why don't the righteous prosper? Why do the wicked succeed? Why do the innocent suffer, while the guilty go free? Why does God allow evil people to prosper at the expense of good people? Or, more personally, if being a Christian is supposed to help me succeed and prosper in this life, why hasn't it? I hope you'll consider carefully several possible answers to that question.

7

A MATTER OF PERCEPTION

Concerning why Christians don't prosper, we need to consider the possibility that many disciples really prosper more than they realize. Their feeling that they are not prospering—that they are not doing well financially—may be more a matter of perception than of reality. We all know that the idea of being rich and being poor is, like beauty, in "the eye of the beholder." How many times have you heard people of an older generation—the generation that lived through the Great Depression—say something like, "Oh yes, we were poor, but we didn't know it, because we were just like everybody else." Those folks were likely to go on to say something like, "We did all right. We had food on the table, a place to sleep, clothes to wear to school. We got milk from our cow, and eggs from our chickens. We thought we were well off." Even today there are people who have little material wealth but don't seem to mind it. I remember reading a few years ago that someone surveyed citizens of many of the countries of the world to see in which country the people were happiest. It turned out, as I recall, that the people of Bangladesh, one of the poorest countries on earth, were the happiest people in the world!

How can you explain the fact that poor people can be happy? One explanation is that "rich" and "poor" are matters of perception, and we perceive ourselves to be "rich" or "poor" compared to other people we know.[1] So our parents (or grandparents or great-grandparents) were satisfied though they were (by modern standards) poor because they compared themselves with those about them—who had the same amount they had. And, we might say, the people of Bangladesh are happy maybe because they have not learned to want as much as we think we have to have, and maybe because the people they know have no more than they have.

So in the modern United States, whom do we "know"? Thanks to modern media—newspapers, magazines, radio, television, the internet, and, especially, social media—we think we know the billionaire business tycoons, the millionaire actors and ballplayers, the Wall Street bankers, and the rich people in our own communities. We see these people living in luxury, and—even if we are doing well in our own occupation—we feel like paupers in comparison. In addition, we live in a materialistic society which shouts at us: "IF YOU DON'T HAVE THE LATEST AUTOMOBILE, LIVE IN A $500,000 HOME, TAKE VACATIONS IN EUROPE, AND WEAR A BIG DIAMOND RING, YOU'RE POOR!" Not only that, but materialism says, "You're out of it; you're nothing, you're useless."

---

1. In an email, Glen McMillan, who owned an automobile dealership before he retired, and who has presented a series on stewardship to several congregations, said, "I used to explain that very few consider themselves rich. [A rich person] is always [someone] we perceive as having more than we do, and those who have less [we see as] lazy." Glen McMillan, email to Coy Roper, December 23, 2015.

Faced with these facts—the inevitability of our comparing ourselves with the richest among us, and the persistence of the materialistic tradition in the United States—it is no wonder that Christians often feel dissatisfied with their own situation. No wonder that, if we don't live in a mansion or make six figures a year or if we still owe money on our house or car, we don't feel that we are prospering. If we are dissatisfied with what we have, maybe we should follow Paul's example. He said, "And having food and clothing, with these we shall be content" (1 Tim 6:8). And "I have learned in whatever state I am, to be content" (Phil 4:11).

However, more pertinent for our purposes is the fact that our perception can be wrong. Although we may not have much compared to a millionaire, we may be doing quite well compared to the average person in our society. And if we have problems that seem to hold us back in this life, it just may be that we don't have as many problems or as severe problems as those who don't practice Christ's way. Add to that the fact that, if we look at our physical wellbeing from a global perspective, a majority of Americans are rich compared to the people who live in many other countries.

So if you are inclined to say, "Christians don't prosper; I know, because I'm a Christian and I haven't prospered," you need to ask yourself this question. Is my lack of prosperity real? Or is it just a matter of perception?

8

THE RESULT OF HUMAN WEAKNESS

If Christians generally prosper, why is it that some don't? Or why is it that we all have problems—financial and otherwise—some of the time? I have said that our feeling that we are not doing well may be a matter of perception. But not always. Sometimes every Christian (like virtually everyone else on the planet) falls short of his or her aspirations and consequently feels frustrated. Why does such a thing happen to Christians who are supposed to be blessed by God? One reason undoubtedly is that we sometimes fail to prosper because of our own human weaknesses. All human beings are fallible. We all make mistakes. If we are willing to admit this, then we should be able to see that many times our failure to prosper is the consequence of our own shortcomings. Our human weaknesses result in two kinds of problems, both of which may get in the way of our material success.

Errors in Judgment

Being human, we all make errors in judgment. If we were on a television game show, we might pick the door that disappoints rather than the one with the prize behind it.

How many people have you heard say, "If only I had bought that land (on which oil was later discovered) when I had the chance"? Drivers hit the accelerator rather than the brake and have accidents. People are human, and because they are human they are imperfect. They make mistakes. However, the consequences of such mistakes are often suffering and failure—both of which are the antitheses of success.

Consequently, if one has not succeeded—if he or she has not prospered as much as they would like—maybe the first thing one ought to do is ask: "What did I do, or fail to do, that brought about my present sorry circumstances?"

Sinful Behavior

Christians may also fail to prosper simply because they fail to live as Christians. By definition, a Christian is one who follows Christ. Following Christ requires one to follow His instructions as found in the Scriptures. When Christians fail to succeed, sometimes it's because they are not living as Christ directs.

If you bought a book entitled "An Infallible Guide to Wealth: Seven Steps to Becoming a Millionaire," do you think it would do you any good if you only read it? Wouldn't you have to do what it says before you could expect it to make you rich? Similarly, we have said that Christians prosper because, in part, they work hard, obey the law, practice Christian virtues, and live as good stewards of what God has entrusted to their care. What if a Christian doesn't work hard? What if he or she breaks the law? What if, rather than being kind and loving and forgiving, one is mean and nasty and antagonistic and vengeful? What if we waste our money and mistreat our bodies? Are we likely to prosper? In other words, just being a Christian will not automatically produce prosperity. Rather, living like a Christian is likely to lead to prosperity. The problem is that we are all human. And humans not only make mistakes, but we all sin (Rom 3:23). And sin has consequences.

Sin's primary consequence is death (Rom 6:23)—spiritual death (separation from God) now, and, unless repented of, eternal death hereafter. In addition, sin has consequences in this life. "Be sure your sin will find you out" (Num 32:23b). David's sin with Bathsheba was forgiven, but he had to suffer the consequences of that sin for the rest of his life (2 Sam 12:10). Those who sin by leaving the Father are likely, like the prodigal, to find themselves in a pigpen (Luke 15). They can be forgiven, as the prodigal was, but their time in the pigpen will not be erased.

In our time we have all seen it happen. A preacher of the gospel in a moment of weakness commits adultery. Consequently, the preacher is disgraced, loses his job, and loses his family. A Christian business owner goes to jail because he or she committed fraud. A church secretary is caught stealing money from the church treasury. A college president driving under the influence of alcohol has a wreck and kills someone. It may be, therefore, that if Christians fail to prosper, it is because they did more than merely make a mistake. It may be that such failures involved sin. Maybe, without intending to, someone becomes addicted to drugs or alcohol. Maybe in anger someone lashes out at someone and hurts them. Maybe someone commits fornication or adultery. Maybe in a moment of fear and anxiety, someone gives in to temptation and lies on a test or steals something that belonged to another. Such sins can condemn us. They can also prevent us from succeeding and from prospering.

But There's Good News

However, if our human weakness has kept us from prospering, there's some good news. The good news is that such problems will not necessarily keep us from doing well in the future. That doesn't mean that we can quit being human and therefore quit making mistakes. As long as we are in the flesh we will make mistakes, and we will sin (1 John 1:8). What Jesus said is still true: "The spirit is willing, but the flesh is weak" (Matt 26:41b). Nevertheless, we can strive to be wiser—to watch our tongues, to be careful where we step, to learn to be cautious drivers. The longer we live, the more we learn, the fewer mistakes we ought to make. More importantly, we have the assurance that we can be forgiven for our sins—no matter how bad they might have been. And when we have turned to Christ and been forgiven, we can start anew, with a clean, fresh slate. Then—if we haven't done it before—we can begin to live as Christ directs, and we can expect blessings to follow. Of course, there may still be consequences to pay because of our past sins. But we can learn to live with those consequences, and, believing that Jesus has something for us to do, press on to make the best of the years we have left.

I said above that suffering and failure are the antitheses of success. That's not necessarily true. If we repent of our sins, and learn from our mistakes, even our negative experiences can open doors to us which we never knew existed. Many have learned that suffering and failure, rather than ruining their chances for success, have provided opportunities for them to succeed—in ways that benefitted themselves and blessed others. People who were themselves once addicted have become adept at helping others overcome addiction. Former inmates have initiated productive prison ministries. People who have overcome psychological problems have become effective counselors. Perhaps you might see your own suffering and failures, not just as something to be overcome and forgotten, but as something that will enable you to become a more effective helper and a more proficient worker for the Lord.

Conclusion

Still, the major point I have been trying to make remains true. Sometimes when Christians don't prosper it's because of their own weaknesses. They either make mistakes or errors in judgment or they give in to temptation and sin. When they do, if they want to know whose fault it is that they are faring so badly, all they have to do is to look in the mirror.

Yet in other cases the causes of our failures seem to lie outside ourselves. What if we have problems that are not of our own making? If it's not our fault that we don't prosper, what can we do about it? We'll consider that question in the next chapter.

9

THE WORKING OF GOD'S WILL

The reaction of many readers to the theme of this chapter may be like that of the disciples who said of Jesus' claim to be the bread of life: "This is a hard saying; who can hear it?" (John 6:60b, KJV). If a Christian does not prosper, it may be because it is the will of God. Christians nowadays don't want to hear such an assertion or to entertain such a possibility. Strangely, if I were to say that Christians sometimes don't prosper because of bad luck . . . or because of chance . . . or because things simply don't go their way . . . or because of their peculiar circumstances . . . many would nod their heads in agreement. Some wouldn't mind even if I said, "Some Christians don't prosper because of fate, or because of bad karma."

But they don't like to give God the "credit" (or blame) for the problems they have. Presumably they believe that since "God is love," He could not and would not deliberately cause, or allow, His people to experience, through no fault of their own, failure or suffering or sorrow or personal problems. God intended for His people to be happy, they believe, so how could He be the source of circumstances that cause them unhappiness or keep them from succeeding? Consequently, they are inclined to reject the idea that bad things happen—or that good things fail to happen—to us because of the working of God's will. Are they right? I want to try to answer that question, but let's begin with a proposition that everyone can agree on.

Sometimes Our Failures Are Not Our Own Fault

In the last chapter I made the point that frequently people fail to succeed, and so to prosper, because of their own weaknesses. Maybe they make mistakes in judgment and those mistakes cost them dearly. Maybe they sin, and, for them, the "wages of sin" include failure in this life. But everyone knows that sometimes we experience problems—problems which result in our failing to succeed in our personal life or in our business life or in our social life—*through no fault of our own*. For example, we may suffer and fail to succeed because of one of the following.

Bad Luck

Our letter gets lost in the mail and we don't get the dream job we always hoped for. A recession comes and we find ourselves unemployed because our job is eliminated. A farmer experiences drought, harvests no crops, and consequently loses the farm.

Workplace Injustices

Many of us believe that we have been fired, or not rehired, unjustly. Others have been passed over, or even demoted, when they deserved a promotion.

Disease and Disability

Disease and disability cause suffering and hinder achievement. Hardly ever can anyone say a sick or disabled person deserves his or her problem.

Accidents

Accidents take lives, cripple people, destroy property—and often they are unavoidable and/or the innocent suffer along with the guilty.

Natural Disasters

Those affected did nothing to cause their suffering from floods, landslides, tornadoes, tsunamis, etc.

Consequences of Crime

Criminals hurt others. They prey on innocent people. Their victims cannot be blamed for their misfortune. And their misfortune will probably detract from their prosperity.

Being the Target of Another's Malice

Sadly, people sometimes suffer and fail to succeed because they—for no good reason—become the target of some malicious person. Being lied about, criticized, scorned, ridiculed, ignored, or bullied is not enjoyable and can prevent one's success. People—including Christians—often fail to succeed, and thus fail to prosper, for one or more of these reasons.

So we can all agree that sometimes our success or failure is a matter of situations over which we have no control. Christians may not prosper, therefore, because of the circumstances of their birth, or because they were a victim of crime, or because they contracted a disease or became disabled, or because their house was swept away in a flood, or because they were unjustly fired, or because they were simply in the wrong place at the wrong time. Is there more to be said? People look for purpose and meaning in their lives, and Christians surely want to believe that the things that happen to them happen for a reason. The fact is that they do, though the reason may not be readily apparent. How do I know? Because:

God Is at Work in the World

Christians should rejoice that God is not only looking down on us from heaven, but He is also active in the world. He not only created the universe but also "upholds" it (Heb 1:2, 3). He is everywhere (Psa 139:7–10). He is "above all and through all and in you all" (Eph 4:6), and He is "not far from each one of us; for in Him we live and move and have our being" (Acts 17:27, 28). He works through providence to bring about good from the things that happen to His saints (Rom 8:28). Consequently, nothing happens without His at least allowing it to happen. In that sense, the Bible pictures Him as the cause of everything—including things which we count as good and things which we see as bad. For instance, it is God who makes a man "mute or deaf, or seeing or blind" (Exod 4:11, NASB). Thus, it could be said that whatever happens is a result, at least, of the permissive will of God.[1] Two examples may help us understand that fact.

When Joseph revealed himself to his brothers in Egypt, they were afraid he would take vengeance on them for the wrong they had done him, but he said, "God sent me before you to preserve life" (Gen 45:5). Later he told them, "You meant evil against me, but God meant it for good, in order to bring it about as it is this day, to save many people alive" (Gen 50:20). "God is responsible," Joseph said, "for this present state of affairs." Think about that. What had brought about the circumstances in which Joseph and his brothers found themselves?

In the story of Joseph . . .

- sinful behavior (on the part of the brothers and Potiphar's wife),
- human strengths—hard work and wise suggestions (on Joseph's part),

---

1. We are distinguishing between the "permissive" will of God, and the "perfect" will of God. The "perfect" will of God is that which He desires to happen and that which He requires of us. For example, God wills that all be saved (Ezek 18:32; 33:11; 2 Pet 3:9). The "permissive" will of God refers to what He permits, to what He allows to happen, even if it is not according to His "perfect" will, even if it happens as a result of sinful acts. So even though He desires for all to be saved, He permits men to have free will, and to be tempted, and so to be lost, if they choose to refuse His grace. We should add that the "will of God" is at work in the world to accomplish His purposes, in accordance with His plans for individuals, for humankind, and for the planet; but we cannot know—we can only guess at—His plans and purposes for us and for the world (other than what He has revealed in His word, the Bible).

- righteous behavior (Joseph's refusal to sin with Potiphar's wife),
- societal customs (the brothers' selling Joseph to traders going to Egypt who then sold him to Potiphar),
- fortuitous circumstances (Joseph "just happened" to be sent by his father; the traders "just happened" to pass by at the right moment; the butler and baker "just happened" to be thrown into prison at the right time),
- "acts of nature" (seven years of plenty, seven years of famine),
- God's divine intervention (through dreams and their interpretation) . . .

. . . combined together to bring about the results in the story.

But Joseph said: "God did it!" God used all these things to bring about the desired results in Joseph's story.

The story of Job provides another example of the fact that God can be "credited with" (or blamed for) whatever happens. Though natural disasters, the sinful acts of evil men, and undeserved sickness, caused (though Job did not know it) by Satan's attacks had robbed him of his possessions and his children, he cried, "Naked I came from my mother's womb, and naked shall I return there. The Lord gave, and the Lord has taken away; blessed be the name of the Lord" (Job 1:21). We might respond: "What did you say, Job? Didn't the wicked Sabeans take your donkeys? Didn't lightning kill your sheep? Didn't the Chaldeans steal your camels? Didn't the great wind destroy your house and kill all your children? Who took it all away from you?" Job would reply: "The Lord has taken [it all] away." God did it! We might add that when God later spoke to

Job and his friends, He never reproached Job for blaming Him (or giving Him credit) for all the bad things that had happened to him.

These passages illustrate the biblical viewpoint: (1) God is always present and at work in the world, and (2) nothing happens without God's permission. Unless God allows it to happen, nothing happens.[2]

Our Lives Are Affected by God's Will

Early Christians understood that fact. Paul wrote to the Corinthians, "I will come to you shortly, if the Lord wills" (1 Cor 4:19; see also Acts 21:14; Rom 1:10; 15:32). Peter said that a Christian's suffering because of persecution could be attributed to the will of God: "For it is better, if it is the will of God, to suffer for doing good than for doing evil" (1 Pet 3:17; see also 1 Pet 4:19). And James wrote,

> Come now, you who say, 'Today or tomorrow we will go to such and such a city, spend a year there, buy and sell, and make a profit'; whereas you do not know what will happen tomorrow. For what is your

---

2. However, we need to make it clear that God does not sin, nor does He cause man to sin (Jam 1:13). The devil is the great tempter. It is he who tempts men by appealing to their lusts (Jam 1:14, 15). Still God is involved in temptation and sinning, because He gives people free will, thus permitting them to sin, and He gives the devil, the tempter, access to people, allowing him freedom to tempt human beings. Nevertheless, the Lord is all-powerful and the devil is not. Thus, the Lord places limits on how far the devil can go in tempting people to sin (1 Cor 10:13; see the limits God placed on Satan in the book of Job).

life? It is even a vapor that appears for a little time and then vanishes away. Instead you ought to say, 'If the Lord will, we shall live and do this or that.' (Jam 4:13-15).

In other words, God determines, through the working of His will, whether we will be allowed to carry out our plans or not.

To affirm that, in a sense, all that happens is the result of the working of God's will does not take away from the fact that humans have free moral agency. God gave each person free will. He does not predetermine what we will do in any particular circumstance. We have freedom to make our decisions, for good or ill. Rather, it means that God—in ways we cannot foresee, understand, or explain—can take the decisions we have freely made and providentially weave them together with other elements in our circumstances—"accidental" occurrences or "natural" forces, for instance—to produce a tapestry that looks how He wants it to look.

Since God's will is at work in our lives, if we run into impenetrable walls, or are decimated by personal losses, or experience a crippling disease so that we do not accomplish what we had hoped to accomplish, we can biblically and truthfully say that it happened because of the working of God's will. Which is not to say that other factors were not involved—sins, mistakes, "bad luck," coming into contact with pernicious germs, the evil acts of evil people—but behind it all was God. He chose to allow these things to happen to us, just as He allowed Joseph and Job to suffer. If we can agree that this is the biblical view, still another question needs answering. How should we react to knowing that God's will is at work in our lives?

The Working of God's Will Gives Meaning to Our Lives

The Christian has an advantage over the unbeliever. When something happens for (apparently) no good reason, the unbeliever can only (consistently) say that such is what one ought to expect from a meaningless universe. In contrast, the Christian can say, "What happened to me was strange and unexpected and disappointing. I don't understand it and can't explain it, but I believe that 'all things work together for good' to those who are called according to God's purpose" (Rom 8:28). Thus, the accident that tore up his car may provide an opportunity for a Christian to make new friends. The disease that crippled a person may turn him or her in a new direction where even more good will be accomplished. Losing everything in a terrible catastrophe may cause someone to see the futility of materialism and the necessity of turning to Christ and spiritual values. Failure in one endeavor may lead to success in another. In any case, whatever happens, Christians can take comfort from the belief that God is at work in this world and in their lives. So even those negative things that happen to us which keep us from success and prosperity—even those negative things can be used by God to accomplish His purposes through our lives.

Therefore, the problems we have which are not our fault and which keep us from fulfilling our dreams may be part of God's greater plan for our lives. And maybe He knows, better than we do, what is best for us. Our response to whatever happens should be to "give thanks" in everything (1 Thess 5:17), to pray "thy will be done" (Matt 6:10, KJV), and to seek God's guidance in determining what we should do next.

Conclusion

This advice is hard to swallow, especially when it seems to us that God has somehow willed for someone else to live off the fat of the land while we flounder in the sewers. How can we accept God's will when it seems to be so arbitrarily unfair?

Three answers to that question come to mind. First, if we are going to accuse God of unfairness, we need to be consistent. Why was God so unfair to allow you to be born in a prosperous country instead of one where poverty is the rule? We don't complain of God's unfairness when we are on the receiving end of God's blessings (which others do not receive). Why should we complain when we are not blessed as others are?

Second, do you think you could run the universe better than God? That's another way of saying that "God's ways are past finding out." We cannot completely understand them—no one can—all we can do is accept them. And until we can prove that we are smarter than God, we would be wise to accept the way He does things.

Third, it is better to have a Christian attitude towards those who do better than we do. A Christian attitude will cause you to rejoice with those who rejoice (Rom 12:15), even when God has prospered them more than He has prospered you. To fail to do so makes it look like you are envious or jealous. To do so provides a way for you to feel good about yourself, while you make others feel good also. Questions about why God wills that some should prosper more than I do will arise, but they should not dominate my thinking or keep me from praising God.

10

BECAUSE THEY CHOOSE NOT TO

I have said that, even though Christians generally prosper, sometimes they don't. When they don't do well financially, it may be a matter of perception (really they are doing better than they think), or it may be because of their own mistakes or sins, or it may be the result of the working of God's will in their lives. God allows them to fail even though they have done nothing to deserve failure. There's another possible explanation for some Christians' failure to succeed materially. They may simply choose not to. There are members of religious orders who take a vow of poverty. I'm not recommending such vows. Nevertheless, sometimes Christians deliberately make choices which dictate that they will probably never be among society's elite.

At least two kinds of deliberate choices might keep a Christian from prospering or at least appearing to prosper. Imagine a young man or a young woman with all the intelligence and skills and talent and drive required to make it big in the business world. He or she could become, if they chose to, the CEO of a Fortune 500 company. Their parents and teachers wait with bated breath to learn what their talented child or student will do with all that ability. But the young man or woman says, "I'm going to be a missionary." Not going to M.I.T. or Harvard? Not going to become a brain surgeon or a nuclear physicist or an astronaut? Not planning to become a bank president or company CEO?

Why would anyone do such a thing? Whatever the reason, talented people—who might otherwise use their talents to accumulate wealth for themselves—have often rejected that alternative to dedicate themselves to helping others and/or to spreading God's word. So they have become nurses and teachers and social workers and workers in children's homes and preachers and missionaries, etc.—when they might have sought jobs which were much more financially rewarding. I am not saying that the people who choose such careers are never paid a living wage. Nor am I saying that they never prosper. Sometimes through careful management (and with God's blessing) they do as well as people in other, more lucrative, occupations. Nor am I saying that those who choose careers which promise greater financial rewards are necessarily motivated by sinful desires. What I am saying is that sometimes talented people purposely choose vocations which promise fewer monetary rewards than they might expect to make in more remunerative jobs. Thus, they fail to prosper to some extent because they choose not to.

Other Christians, whatever their occupation, deliberately choose a lifestyle that does not reflect their prosperous financial status. They make big bucks, but they live like "ordinary people." You might expect them to drive a Cadillac or a Lincoln or a Mercedes-Benz, but they get by with a ten-year-old Toyota. Why? There are some people like Dickens' Ebenezer Scrooge who can't bear to spend a nickel unless they have to, so they squirrel their money away "for a rainy day." We've all heard of folks who lived like paupers, but when they died their neighbors discovered that they were worth millions. These are not the kind of people I'm talking about. I'm talking about people who choose to live at a much lower socio-economic level than they can afford, so that they can give more to the Lord and to others. They desire to do good with their money rather than spending it on creature comforts for themselves. For example, I once heard about a family in Georgia. They were very well off but chose to live in a small house without central air conditioning so that they could give most of their income to good causes. An outsider, seeing such a family, would conclude that they were not prosperous. But their lack of prosperity—or the appearance thereof—would be a matter of choice. Many Christians choose to live below the lifestyle their income would allow in order that they might do more good with their money. The question remains. Why?

Why Choose Not to Prosper?

Why would a Christian make such choices? We live in a society in which people are often judged by how much they make, how big their house is, what kind of clothes they wear, what kind of car they drive, where they go on vacation (to Paris, France or to Paris, Texas), whether they are members of the local country club, etc. Anyone who doesn't measure up to these standards is usually regarded as ordinary, or even useless, by many of society's elite.[1] So why would anyone deliberately choose to drop out of the rat race? To reject the possibility that he or she might

---

1. This is an overstatement, of course. In many cities and communities, good citizens are often recognized for their service to others even though they may not themselves be affluent. Nevertheless, the trend of modern society is to hold up the rich as the ideal for which all should strive.

ever measure up to the standards of success accepted by the majority of one's fellow citizens?

There's really only one answer to that question. Before folks can choose to reject the attainment of riches as their goal in life, they must reject the standards—the measuring stick—of the world. Many have rejected worldly standards for higher purposes. I knew of a young man who had been a student at Michigan Christian College (now Rochester College) when I taught there who gave up a job in business making more than $100,000 a year to become a preacher for less than half that salary. Today Christians who choose to become preachers and missionaries, knowing that their vocational choice will ensure that they never get rich, do so because they value the spiritual over the material. To them, saving souls is more important than making (a lot of) money. Likewise, Christians who choose service-oriented occupations (like teaching, nursing, counseling, social work) show that they are more interested in helping people than in getting rich. And Christians who live below their means in order to give to good causes indicate that they are willing to put others before themselves. All of them demonstrate what it means to obey Jesus' words: "Do not lay up for yourselves treasures on earth, where moth and rust destroy, and where thieves break in and steal; but lay up for yourselves treasures in heaven, where neither moth nor rust destroys, and where thieves do not break in and steal" (Matt 6:19, 20).

Conclusion

Usually Christians do well in our society. If they don't, it may be because of mistakes they have made or because of circumstances beyond their control. Or it may be that they simply choose not to prosper—at least not by this world's standards. They march, we might say, to the beat of a different drummer. They don't worry about whether they prosper, or appear to prosper. Their aim is to serve the Lord and help humankind. They don't particularly expect to receive a reward here for doing so, but they expect to be rewarded in heaven. Whether or not they prosper in the here and now matters little to them. It just may be that sometimes a Christian's lack of material prosperity may be evidence of his or her spiritual prosperity.

PART 3

WHY IT DOESN'T MATTER

In part one of this book, I said that under normal circumstances most Christians will prosper financially, compared to others in their community and to what they might be able to accomplish if they were not Christians or did not live by Christian standards. Why? Because the requirements of God's laws are really good for us. They help us succeed and live an abundant life.

In part two I said that Christians sometimes don't prosper (or appear to prosper) materially for several reasons. However, even when things go badly for the faithful Christian he or she can believe that God is working, and will work, even through the adverse circumstances of life to bring about a favorable outcome (from God's standpoint).

In this section of the book I want to add another word about financial or material success. If we are devoted disciples of Christ, it doesn't (or shouldn't) make much difference to us whether or not we prosper. Don't get me wrong. There is some value in succeeding—financially and otherwise—in this life. But the main thing Christians are (or ought to be) concerned about is not how we are doing in business, or how much money we have in the bank, but in how we are doing spiritually.

So in these final pages I urge all of us to see material success, prosperity, and financial security in its proper perspective. In some ways becoming well off may be important, but it is not nearly as important as making your "calling and election sure" (2 Pet 1:10, KJV). From an eternal standpoint it may make no difference at all whether you are rich or poor, whether you are prosperous or not. It's that standpoint I want you to consider in the following chapters.

11

IT DOES MATTER

I have defined "prosperity" in terms of material prosperity. In this section of the book I will be arguing that it doesn't really matter whether a Christian prospers materially or not. But before I can elaborate on that thesis, I need to qualify it. There are some ways in which it does matter whether a Christian prospers financially—at least to some extent.

To Support Your Family

The New Testament does not require Christians to be so focused on heaven as to be of no earthly use. In fact, Christians are required to work for a living (Eph 4:28). One reason they are to work is to support their own families—including their extended families (which would include their parents and grandparents, their aunts and uncles, etc.); see 1 Tim 5:8. Thus, every Christian needs to find a way to make enough money to meet his or her own needs and the needs of close family. No Christian is justified in deliberately choosing to live on handouts from others rather than to work for a living (2 Thess

3:10).[1] Consequently Christians must do their best to prosper to the extent that they can meet their own needs and the needs of their close relatives.

To Support the Church

Christians are required to work to feed their families but that's not all. Ephesians 4:28 says that each Christian must "labor, working with his hands what is good, that he may have something to give him has need." Christians work, not to have or to buy or to save, but to give. A primary objective of a Christian's work is to give to those who are in need.

In New Testament times Christians freely shared their goods with others (see Acts 2–5). Churches collected contributions from their members in order to help poor saints. And Christians were commanded to give of their means on the first day of the week in order to help meet the needs of others (1 Cor 16:1, 2).

Today the church follows the New Testament pattern by taking up a collection from its members on the first day of every week. From that collection, it pays its expenses, supports the preaching of the gospel, does benevolent work, and helps missionaries spread God's word among people of other cultures and countries.

But what if every member of the church took a vow of poverty? How could the good works that God expects us to do, individually and as a church, get done? Who would pay for a place for the saints to meet? Who would pay the preacher's

---

1. Obviously this sentence does not describe one who is unable to work for some reason and so receives support from others. Such a person does not deliberately choose a life of sloth and dependency.

salary? How could benevolent programs be sustained? Who would send the missionaries "into all the world"? Unless most of the members of a congregation are working and making a living wage, and giving to the Lord as He requires, many of the works of the church will go undone. Therefore, Christians need to prosper to the extent that they can give enough to help the church do the work God has assigned to it.

To Give to Good Works

Most of the members of the first century church were not rich. Paul said that "not many wise according to the flesh, not many mighty, not many noble" had become Christians at Corinth (1 Cor 1:26). However, that verse implies that at least some who were wise, noble, and mighty had accepted Jesus. The New Testament provides evidence of the fact that in the church there were some who were in what we might call the upper class. Erastus, a city treasurer, was a Christian (Rom 16:23). Mary, the mother of John Mark, had a house large enough for the church to meet in to pray for Peter (Acts 12:12). In Thessalonica some of the leading women were converted (Acts 17:4). Paul speaks of some Christians who were rich (1 Tim 6:17-19).

Today most Christians in the United States are what I have called prosperous, but they are not rich. Nevertheless, some are. And those Christians who have made lots of money have often given generously to good causes. They have contributed to children's homes, Christian colleges, mission work, benevolent programs, and to local congregations. Many have privately helped meet the needs of poorer brothers and sisters in Christ. If they had not prospered more than most people, many good works could not have been accomplished.

Conclusion

In what follows, then, I am not asserting that, from a practical standpoint, it makes absolutely no difference whether Christians prosper at all. Christians need to make enough money to meet the needs of their families and to support the work of the church—and the church (and society) is blessed when very prosperous disciples give generously to good causes. But whether a Christian prospers or not does not matter as much as most of us think. Prosperity isn't bad if we keep it in perspective. The drive to prosper materially becomes a problem when it eclipses our spiritual concerns. To the Christian prosperity matters (for the reasons given above), but not nearly as much as most people think.

12

CONTENTMENT

One reason why whether they prosper or not doesn't, or shouldn't, matter to Christians is that the New Testament teaches them to be content. In our consumer-oriented society there is probably no command that is harder for most of us to obey than the command to be content. Everywhere we turn we are confronted with commercials which have one theme—you should be discontented. Your wardrobe is not good enough, so buy some new clothes. Your old car won't do, so you need a new one. Are you satisfied with your life? You shouldn't be. You need this product to make your life complete. Commercials are designed to create or kindle desires—which is to say, to create discontentment and show how the products they are selling will satisfy those desires and bring contentment (until the next commercial comes along).

So the strangest advice to hear in today's world is the directive to be content. Nevertheless, that's what the Lord requires. Listen to the following scriptures:

> Luke 3:14 — "Likewise the soldiers asked him, saying, 'And what shall we do?' So he said to them, 'Do not intimidate anyone or accuse falsely, and be content with your wages.'"

Philippians 4:11b–13 — "... I have learned in whatever state I am, to be content: I know how to be abased, and I know how to abound. Everywhere and in all things I have learned both to be full and to be hungry, both to abound and to suffer need. I can do all things through Christ who strengthens me."

1 Timothy 6:6–8 — "Godliness with contentment is great gain. For we brought nothing into this world, and it is certain we can carry nothing out. And having food and clothing, with these we shall be content."

Hebrews 13:5 — "Let your conduct be without covetousness, and be content with such things as you have. For He Himself has said, 'I will never leave you nor forsake you.'"

No one, after reading these passages, can reasonably deny the proposition that God expects His children today to be content with what they have and to be content in their circumstances. What does it mean to be content, and how, in our commercialized world, can we find contentment?

What Does It Mean to be Content?

Before we can understand what it means to be content, we need to think about what it does not mean. For the Christian being content does not rule out the possibility of having dreams and desires. Nor does it make it wrong to formulate objectives and make plans to achieve them. Paul said that he "had learned to be content," but Paul was one who made plans for the future and who sought to use the best methods possible to accomplish his goals. To be content, therefore, does not require one to be satisfied with his or her education. Nor would it keep someone from looking for a better job to do more for the Lord and to provide more help for others. However, it would require one to accept the outcomes of those efforts with tranquility—even when things don't work out as he or she had hoped.

When the New Testament speaks of contentment, it is not talking about being satisfied with where one is spiritually. The same Paul who said that he was always content also said, in the same book, "I do not count myself to have apprehended; but one thing I do, forgetting those things which are behind and reaching forward to those things which are ahead, I press toward the goal for the prize of the upward call of God in Christ Jesus" (Phil 3:13, 14). The fact is we should never be satisfied with our own spiritual growth. We should always be striving to love more, to do more good, to give more, to become kinder, to better control our thoughts, to do a better job of overcoming temptation and avoiding sin, etc. As far as our spirituality is concerned, we should never be content. We should always be trying to become more like Jesus.

Being content with what you have does not rule out the possibility of feeling compassion for the poor and helpless or indignation concerning sin and wrongdoing. Jesus was angry about the hardheartedness of some (Mark 3:5), wept when a friend died (John 11:35), and lamented the fact that some had rejected Him (Matt 23:37–39). Paul wanted his Jewish family to be saved (Rom 10:1). And when he saw Athens, a city full of idols, his "spirit was provoked within him" (Acts 17:16). Contentment is not hardheartedness. It does not require us to be neutral about ethical questions. It does not rule out compassion for the poor and unfortunate, or a feeling of indignation when we see the helpless mistreated. A Christian should be content but still desire to right the wrongs in the world. Christian contentment always has to do with one's physical or financial situation. The requirement of the command deals specifically with the subject of this book. Whether he or she prospers or not, the Christian should be content.

- If you make plans to be a doctor, but don't get admitted to medical school and end up teaching science in high school, be content.
- If you're preaching for a small church, without much pay, and apply for a job at a larger congregation, but don't get it, be content.
- If you lose a high-paying job and have to go to work for a much lower salary, be content.
- If you find yourself shipwrecked, or stoned and left for dead, or imprisoned for your faith, like Paul, be content.

In other words, Christians, by our attitudes and actions, show the world that whether we prosper or not makes little or no difference. Regardless of our circumstances, we will "rejoice in the Lord always" (Phil 4:4; 1 Thess 5:16), "pray without ceasing" (1 Thess 5:17), and "in everything give thanks" (1 Thess 5:18) knowing that as a result "the peace of God, which surpasses all understanding" will "guard" our hearts and minds "through Christ Jesus" (Phil 4:7).

Content in All Circumstances?

It's hard to be content in a world where the motto is "More!" And it's hard to be content with our circumstances when we always want, not only to have more, but also to achieve more. It's interesting that the context for Paul's well-known affirmation "I can do all things through Him who strengthens me" is his statement "I have learned to be content in whatever state I am." Notice that Paul said, "I have learned . . ." Being content didn't necessarily come easily to Paul. He had to learn to do it. How was he able to learn? Maybe only through the power of Christ. So he said, "I have learned . . . I can do all things," meaning, "I can even learn to be content because of the Christ who strengthens me."

In a similar way, though it may be difficult for us to learn to be content, we can do it because of Christ who strengthens us. How can we do it? If we can remember what is most important in life, we are more likely to be content no matter what happens. If we lose our job, we still have our health. If our physical health deteriorates, we can be content that our soul is doing well. If we are threatened with death, we can look forward to being with Jesus. Jesus taught His followers not to be anxious about food and clothing because "life [is] more than food and the body more than clothing" (Matt 6:25).

We can be content if we will remember that our Lord is always with us (Matt 28:20; Heb 13:5) and that God will not allow us to be tempted beyond our ability to resist (1 Cor 10:13). If we put God's kingdom first, He will meet our needs (Matt 6:33) and that all things work together for good (Rom 8:28). We can someday look forward to going to heaven (2 Tim 4:7, 8). When we are tempted to be discouraged, we need to remember that

God answers prayer (Matt 7:7–9; James 1:5; 1 John 5:14). God provides prayer to help us find our way. He also gives us the privilege of being part of the body of Christ, whose members exist to help us when we feel defeated. Knowing that God answers prayers and that we have the saints on our side should help us be content, no matter what happens to us.

Conclusion

To the Christian, whether he or she prospers makes little difference, because the Christian is—or ought to be—content in all circumstances. Again Paul provides a good example. He and Silas were unjustly thrown into prison in Philippi. In the same circumstances, what would you have done? Cried? Begged for mercy? Cursed God because of the injustice of it all? What did they do? About midnight they were "praying and singing hymns to God" (Acts 16:25). (Remember what James said: "Is anyone cheerful? Let him sing psalms" [Jam 5:13].) Content inside a prison cell? That's why I say that to faithful Christians it doesn't matter whether they prosper, because they can be content regardless of what happens to them.

Is it hard to do? Absolutely! I doubt if anyone finds it easy to be content no matter what happens. But is there anything worthwhile that does not require effort? And the effort required to "learn to be content" in all circumstances will be richly rewarded with the "peace that passes understanding."

13

LOVE OF MONEY

"Money may not be all there is, but it's way ahead of whatever is in second place." Such is probably the sentiment of the greater part of the populace. In contrast, the New Testament teaches Christians not to love money. If they don't, then it is likely that it will make little difference whether they prosper or not. To appreciate that fact, let's consider both negative and positive principles taught in the New Testament regarding money or riches.

Negative Teachings About Money or Riches

The New Testament strongly prohibits placing an undue emphasis on money or riches. It is against three things that most people are for.

First, the New Testament is against the love of money. In 1 Timothy 6:6–10, Paul wrote the following to Timothy:

> But godliness with contentment is great gain. For we brought nothing into this world, and it is certain we can carry nothing out. And having food and clothing, with these we shall be content. But those who desire to be rich fall into temptation and a snare, and

into many foolish and harmful lusts which drown men in destruction and perdition. For the love of money is a root of all kinds of evil, for which some have strayed from the faith in their greediness, and pierced themselves through with many sorrows.

In this passage the "love of money" is (1) contrasted with contentment, (2) said to be equivalent to the desire to "get rich," and (3) identified as the cause of all kinds of sins. The expression "love of money" does not refer to our ordinary desire to have enough money to support ourselves and our families and to be able to give to the Lord and help others. It refers instead to the extraordinary desire to have a lot of money or to "get rich." It refers to a lust for money. It speaks of making money one's primary aim in life. Christians are not to love money in that way or to that extent.[1] As David Roper said, "Paul's concern was for those who crave money, those with an obsession regarding money and what it can buy."[2]

Second, Christians are informed that Jesus is against their giving riches first place in their lives. According to Matthew 6:19, Jesus said, "Do not lay up for yourselves treasures on

---

1. Apparently in the first century there were many false teachers who were motivated by a love for money. Paul spoke of some who thought that "godliness is a means of gain" (1 Tim 6:5) and of others who were "empty talkers and deceivers" who taught "things they should not . . . for the sake of sordid gain" ("filthy lucre," KJV; Titus 1:10, 11, NASB). Peter speaks of false teachers who were motivated by "covetousness" (2 Pet 2:3, 14). Paul made it clear that he was not among the preachers motivated by greed by stressing that he supported himself and took no money from those to whom he was preaching at the time (see, among other passages, Acts 20:33–35).

2. David Roper, *1 and 2 Timothy and Titus* in Truth for Today Commentary Series (Searcy, AR: Resource Publications, 2018), 268.

earth, where moth and rust destroy and where thieves break in and steal." Jesus was not teaching that it is absolutely wrong to save some of your money. Rather, He was saying that "treasures on earth" are not nearly as important as "treasures in heaven." Furthermore, it is foolish to make such treasures your priority because they can so easily be lost.

Jesus tried to teach His disciples a similar lesson in Matthew 16:26, where He said, "For what is a man profited if he gains the whole world, and loses his own soul? Or what will a man give in exchange for his soul?" His point is obvious. The soul is much more important than physical riches. One must not therefore neglect the welfare of His soul to accumulate wealth.

The rich young ruler provided an object lesson on the same subject. When he asked what he needed to do to be saved, Jesus first told him to keep the commandments. When he said that he had done so, Jesus told him to sell all that he had and give the money to the poor and then to follow Him. The young man "went away sorrowful, for he had great possessions" (Matt 19:22). Jesus then spoke of how hard it was for a rich person to be saved (Matt 19:23). No doubt the story is found in our Bibles to illustrate the importance of putting Christ first in one's life. Riches must never have priority in the Christian's life. When they do, their absence—the lack of prosperity—will be keenly felt. When riches do not have preeminence, Christians will scarcely notice their absence.

Third, the Bible teaches against covetousness or greed. Jesus said, "Take heed and beware of covetousness, for one's life does not consist in the abundance of the things he possesses" (Luke 12:15). Among the sins which Paul said belonged to the Christian's former life was "covetousness, which is idolatry" (Col 3:5)—and idolatry is one of those sins which will condemn a person for eternity (Rev 21:8). Paul was reiterating the tenth commandment of the Law: "You shall not covet your neighbor's house; you shall not covet your neighbor's wife, nor his manservant, nor his maidservant, nor his ox, nor his donkey, nor anything that is your neighbor's" (Exod 20:17).

The prohibition of covetousness or greed may sound strange in the ears of a twenty-first century American. The capitalistic, free enterprise system may seem to thrive on greed. Gordon Gekko, portrayed by Michael Douglas in the film *Wall Street*, probably stated what is thought to be the ultimate truth regarding our economic system when he said, "Greed is good!" But the Bible teaches otherwise. It teaches that God's people must renounce greed or covetousness.

A covetous or greedy person always want more. He or she wants what their neighbor has—and, as the Old Testament command makes plain, they may want, not just the same kind of thing the neighbor has, but the very thing the neighbor has. They covet it today, and tomorrow they may take steps to steal it. However, the Bible, in both the Old Testament and the New Testament, condemns, not just the theft, but the covetousness which leads to the theft.

But one can be guilty of covetousness without wanting his or her neighbor's stuff. A man asked Jesus to make his brother divide the family inheritance with him. After saying that it was not His business to get involved in the distribution of inheritances, Jesus warned His listeners against "covetousness" (Luke 12:13–15; "every form of greed," NASB). Then Jesus told a story to illustrate His warning. He told about a man who made a great harvest, built bigger barns to store it in, and then said to himself, "Soul, you have many goods laid up for many years to come; take your ease, eat, drink and be merry" (Luke

12:16–19). But that very night God said to him, "You fool! This very night your soul will be required of you; then whose will those things be which you have provided?" Jesus concluded with the words, "So is he who lays up treasure for himself, and is not rich toward God" (Luke 12:20, 21). Jesus' point was that those who are greedy are trying to get where the rich man was—to acquire enough money that they will be assured of an easy life for the rest of their days. However, even if they achieve that aim, they are fools because they have worked for something which they could lose overnight. Covetousness or greed equals foolishness because of the impermanence of riches. What is permanent? What really lasts? The riches of God. To be wise one needs, not to lay up "treasure for himself," but to be "rich toward God."

We are, therefore, not to covet what others have or to "covet" what we have by hoarding it and trusting in it rather than being rich toward God. And if we are not greedy or covetous, we will not be overly concerned about whether our "barns are full." We will instead put our trust in the Lord to meet our needs.

A Positive Passage About Riches

If we are not to love money, to give priority to money, or to covet money, what are we to do about money or riches? To answer that question we want to consider just one passage: 1 Timothy 6:17–19:

> Command those who are rich in this present age not to be haughty, nor to trust in uncertain riches but in the living God, who gives us richly all things to enjoy.

Let them do good, that they may be rich in good works, ready to give, willing to share, storing up for themselves a good foundation for the time to come, that they may lay hold on eternal life.

This passage is interesting because, for one thing, it reveals that there were some (probably not many) rich people in the first century church. For another, it is interesting because it comes almost immediately after Paul has forbidden Christians to love money (v. 10) and has equated the love of money with the desire to "get rich" (v. 9). Either the rich Christians of verse 17 had been converted after they were already rich or, if they had been following Paul's instructions, they became rich without loving money or desiring to get rich. The passage seems to teach that Christians can become rich without sinning if it happens—sort of—accidentally. Actually, it would be better to say that Christians can become rich if that is not their primary aim in life. If their primary aim is to put Christ first, glorify God, and serve people by using the talents God has given them to the full, and the result is that they get rich along the way, then there is nothing wrong with becoming rich.

However, the most significant thing about this passage is what the Lord teaches those who are rich to do. They are to:

- *Not be conceited,* or full of pride, because of their riches. The proper attitude for the Christian, no matter how little or how much he or she has, is humility. We are never worthy of the blessings God gives us.
- *Not trust in their riches.* Christians may be rich, but their trust must not be in money but in God. Why not

trust in riches? Because of their uncertainty. They are here today and gone tomorrow.

- *Be thankful to God,* who has given Christians what they have, for it is He who gives people "all things to enjoy."
- *Do good with what they have*—to be "rich," not just in the money they have in the bank, but "in good works;" and to be "ready to give, willing to share" their good fortune with others.
- *Place their emphasis, not on the riches they have on the earth, but on the "time to come"*—on going to heaven—and enjoying, not what people call "the good life" here, but the "eternal life."

Most Americans could be classified as "rich" compared to much of the rest of the world. Therefore, even if we feel we are just average citizens, we need to ask ourselves whether we should take these words to heart and apply them to our own lives.

For our purposes, however, this passage provides further evidence that, no matter how rich a Christian is, there are some things that are more important than riches. If we follow Paul's advice, money will not be the most important thing in our lives. What matters is being humble and grateful, trusting in God, doing good, and going to heaven. That's what really matters.

Conclusion

The Bible teaches that money is not the be-all and end-all of everything. It is not the sum of our existence. Other things are more important—having friends, for instance, and enjoying good health. And being right with God is far more important. Morally, money is neutral. It can be used for good or evil purposes. The Christian's aim should be, however much money he or she has, to use it for God and for good. And if we have a scriptural understanding of money and riches, we will also understand that whether we have a lot of it, or not much, makes little difference. What makes a difference is not whether we are rich in this life but whether we are rich toward God.

14

DIFFERENT PRIORITIES

A third reason why it doesn't, or shouldn't, matter to Christians whether or not they prosper is that they have an otherworldly value system. They have different priorities than most people. They value the spiritual over the material. They take seriously the following scriptural requirements. "Do not love the world or the things in the world" (1 John 2:15a). "Pure and undefiled religion ... is this ... to keep oneself unspotted from the world" (Jam 1:27). "Do not be conformed to this world" (Rom 12:2a). We are "not of the world" (John 17:16). "Seek those things which are above, where Christ is ... Set your mind on things above, not on things on the earth" (Col 3:1b, 2).

Like the heroes of faith in Hebrews 11, Christians confess that they are "strangers and pilgrims on the earth" (Heb 11:13; see also 1 Pet 2:11). They accept as still true the message of Ecclesiastes, which is that everything that men strive for—worldly accomplishments, riches, wisdom, pleasure, etc.—is, apart from God, "vanity and striving after wind" (Eccl 2:11, NASB); and that in the end the "whole duty of man" is to "fear God and keep his commandments" (Eccl 12:13, KJV). They mean it when they sing, "This world is not my home, I'm just a passing thru."[1] "Earth holds no treasures but perish with using, However precious they be; Yet there's a country to which I am going: Heaven holds all to me."[2]

A Different Set of Values

Christians value spiritual riches over material riches. Being "rich toward God" is more important than storing up treasures for oneself (Luke 12:21). They are like Moses, who chose "rather to suffer affliction with the people of God than to enjoy the passing pleasures of sin, esteeming the reproach of Christ greater riches than the treasures in Egypt; for he looked to the reward" (Heb 11:25, 26). Since "treasures in heaven" are more important to the Christian than "treasures on earth" (Matt 6:19-21), it doesn't make much difference whether he or she is rich or poor in this life.

Christians value spiritual life and health over physical life and health. They know that even if their body deteriorates, their soul can remain healthy and strong. As Paul said, "We do not lose heart, . . . though our outward man is perishing, yet the inward man is being renewed day by day" (2 Cor 4:16; see also Eph 3:16). Of course, one's physical health is important, but to the Christian it is not nearly as important as his spiritual wellbeing. And physical life itself is less significant to the child of God than spiritual life in Christ. If we must choose between maintaining our allegiance to Christ and dying for the faith, we will gladly give up our lives, knowing that "to depart and be with Christ . . . is far better" (Phil 1:23).

---

1. "This World is Not My Home," arranged by Albert E. Brumley.
2. "Earth Holds No Treasures" by Tillit S. Tiddlie.

Christians value God's approval over the approval of others. Writing to the Galatians, Paul expressed the idea eloquently: "Am I now seeking the favor of men, or of God? Or am I striving to please men?" He made it clear that his aim was to please God by adding, "If I were still trying to please men, I would not be a bond-servant of Christ" (Gal 1:10, NASB). To the Thessalonians he said, "We speak, not as pleasing men, but God" (1 Thess 2:4). The desire to please God will prompt them to question the path recommended by others, for they know that "there is a way which seems right to a man, but its end is the way of death" (Prov 14:12).

Almost everyone wants the approval of his or her peers. The Christian, however, knows that something is more important than peer approval—namely, doing the will of God and pleasing Him. Choosing such a course may not make one popular or prosperous, but to a disciple that fact matters far less than faithfully serving his or her Lord.

Christians value their heavenly home over their earthly home. As precious as their earthly home may be to them, that heavenly home to which they are going is even more precious. In that heavenly home, God Himself will be present and will "wipe away every tear from their eyes; and there shall be no more death, nor sorrow, nor crying; and there shall be no more pain" (Rev 21:4).

We are all citizens of an earthly nation, but more importantly to us is the fact that we "seek a homeland," a "better . . . a heavenly country" (Heb 11:14, 16). If circumstances require us, on our journey to that better country, to leave our home, we do so gladly, knowing that being sure that we will live permanently in our heavenly home is more important than our temporary dwelling on this planet.

Christians value their spiritual family over their earthly family. Hopefully, our families will encourage us to be faithful to Christ. If, however, we must choose between following Jesus and remaining with our earthly families, Christians will choose Christ. He said, "If anyone comes to Me and does not hate his father and mother, wife and children, brothers and sisters, yes, and his own life also, he cannot be My disciple" (Luke 14:26).[3] God's family on earth consists of the church (1 Tim 3:15). Christians are members of the church (Acts 2:47; 1 Cor 12:13), and therefore members of God's spiritual family. God is their Father, and they are related to one another as brothers and sisters in Christ, Who claims His disciples as His family members (Mark 3:31–35). Christ loved and died for the church (Eph 5:25). Therefore, Christians can never forsake the church, their spiritual family, even if they are forced to leave their physical family. God's family must be an important part of their life, even though it may not contribute to their financial prosperity.

Christians value God's people over any earthly people or nation. The church is not only Christ's body and God's family. The people of God are also spoken of as God's "holy nation" (1 Pet 2:9). Christians may love their country (and certainly must obey its laws), but their supreme allegiance is not to their country—no matter what country it is—but to the "holy nation" of which they are citizens. At times their loyalty to Christ and God's "holy nation" may make it difficult for them to prosper in their country, but following the Lord faithfully will mean more to them than mindlessly obeying laws contrary to God's will.

---

3. The word "hate" in this passage should be understood to mean "love less."

Christians value heavenly achievements over earthly accomplishments. Almost everyone has ambitions. Folks want to be the greatest ball player, the best musician, the fastest runner, an outstanding actor, or an award-winning scientist. There's nothing wrong with having such ambitions, but the Christian subordinates those ambitions to the desire to be a faithful, productive, disciple of Christ. And, as such, he or she has other, spiritual, more important ambitions. Paul provides a good example of this characteristic. He said, "If anyone else thinks he may have confidence in the flesh, I more so" (Phil 3:4b). Then, after listing his accomplishments, he added,

> But what things were gain to me, these I have counted loss for Christ. But indeed I also count all things loss for the excellence of the knowledge of Christ Jesus my Lord, for whom I have suffered the loss of all things, and count them as rubbish, that I may gain Christ. (Phil 3:7, 8)

Even so, Christians may rejoice in whatever they achieve, but most important are spiritual achievements. If one is in Christ, serving Christ faithfully, and looking forward to living with Christ in another life, worldly successes are, in comparison, "rubbish." Furthermore, the New Testament challenges the Christian to achieve other goals—to put off the "works of the flesh" and to produce the "fruit of the Spirit" (Gal 5:19–26); to "grow in the grace and knowledge of our Lord and Savior Jesus Christ" (2 Pet 3:18); to add Christian virtues to his life (2 Pet 1:5-7); to learn to love as Christ loved (John 13:34, 35); to grow spiritually until he can say with Paul: "It is no longer I who live, but Christ lives in me" (Gal. 2:20). Christians who are naturally ambitious and competitive might make their earthly goals secondary and make spiritual goals primary. Why not have as your major objectives in life the following?

- to be the kindest, most loving person in the community
- to never miss a church service
- to know as much about the Bible as possible
- to never fail to help anyone in need
- to pray daily or even hourly
- to encourage at least one person every day
- to try to reach someone for Christ every week
- to become more and more like Jesus

Christians value their heavenly King, Jesus, over any earthly leader. Jesus is the King of His kingdom (John 18:33–38; Col 1:13). He is, in fact, "King of Kings and Lord of Lords" (1 Tim 6:15). Usually, following our King will not require us to disobey earthly authorities (Rom 13:1; 1 Pet 2:17; Matt 22:17–21). If, however, an earthly authority should require us to disobey Christ's law, like the apostles, "we must obey God rather than men" (Acts 5:29, NASB). To do so may result in our being persecuted rather than prospering, but as Jesus' disciples we have no choice. Regardless of the consequences, we must always obey Christ our King.

Christians value serving others over becoming famous. Many individuals are devoted fans of someone famous. Probably we would all like to be famous, too. From a Christian standpoint, the desire for fame might be questioned. To seek fame is to seek recognition for one's self—to stress the importance of number one. In contrast, the New Testament tells us that Christ gave up His status to humble Himself and come to earth as a servant (Phil 2:6–8). And we are to have the same attitude (Phil 2:5). Christians are to "follow [in Jesus'] steps" (1 Pet 2:21). Christians have as their primary objective in this life not to be recognized for their greatness, but to be a servant of others, just as was their Master (Matt 20:28; John 13:12–17). The Way of Christ is the "way of the cross," not the highway to earthly glory. Unless one is willing to put aside a desire for fame "and deny himself, and take up his cross and follow" Jesus, he or she cannot be Christ's disciple (Matt 16:24). Following Jesus requires one to live a life of service.

Paradoxically, however, Christians are promised the kind of rewards that accompany fame. They can ultimately receive a "crown of righteousness" (2 Tim 4:7, 8). In the letters to the seven churches of Asia in Revelation 2 and 3 Christians who "overcome," who remain faithful to the Lord, are promised, among other things, a "crown of life" (2:10), the "morning star" (2:28), and a place with Christ on His throne (3:21). Christians therefore rejoice, not primarily because their names are found in some sport's record book, or because they have been installed in some Hall of Fame, or have received a "Medal of Honor" or an Academy Award, or because their names are recorded in a "Who's Who" book, but because their names are written in "the Lamb's Book of Life" (Rev 21:27; see also Phil 4:3; Rev 13:8; 20: 12, 15; Luke 10:20). Earthly wealth and fame cannot be our primary goal, but, in a sense, heavenly fame will be our reward for following Christ faithfully.

Christians value eternity in heaven over sinful pleasures on earth. Christians are tempted to sin (Jam 1:13-15). Temptation is strong because sin is pleasurable. Moses rejected the temptation to prosper in Egypt, where he could enjoy the "pleasures of sin" (Heb 11:25). In the parable of the sower, the seed that fell among the thorns represents those who hear the word and obey it, but "they are choked with cares, riches, and pleasures of life, and [so] bring no fruit to maturity" (Luke 8:14). Sin is fun. (Or at least it seems to be.) Why else would people participate in it? Why don't Christians join with others in their sinful activities? Because, for one thing, they know that sin has consequences, even in this life. Prodigals end up in the pigpen. But mainly because they look to their reward in heaven. (See Heb 11:26.) They know that if they will be "faithful until death," abstaining from immorality, they will receive a "crown of life" (Rev 2:10). Going to heaven is more important to them than enjoying, as the KJV says, "the pleasures of sin for a season." Their rejection of sin as a way of life may keep them from prospering, but to them that matters less than spending eternity in heaven.

Caring Little About Whether They Prosper or Not

The Christian's different set of values causes him or her to care little about personal prosperity. If the stock market falls, and a great deal of money is lost, it matters little to the Christian because he or she has "treasures in heaven."

If your parents disown you, you have a heavenly Father to turn to, and brothers and sisters in Christ to console you. If you lose your job, you have the assurance that "all things" will work together "for good" (Rom 8:28) and that Christ will meet your needs (Matt 6:33). If you get sick, you can be thankful that your soul is still strong and healthy. If it seems to you that no one on earth loves you, you can be comforted by knowing that God still loves you. If you are persecuted "for righteousness' sake" you can rejoice, knowing that God will bless you (Matt 5:10) and that God will eventually punish evildoers. What matters most to Christians is obeying their King, not whether others like or dislike them, or praise or persecute them. Obedience to the Lord matters far more than profit or popularity.

When a Christian enters a contest, he or she does their best to win, but if they lose, it matters little, because they know that they can and will win in the end—a crown of life! And when the time comes to die, and leave everything behind, they have no tears for themselves, for they look forward to gaining a home in heaven. In other words, the Christian possesses such blessings and has such hopes, that earthly difficulties—including whether or not one is financially well off—matter little.

Conclusion

Perhaps our greatest challenge as Christians is to reject the usual way of looking at life—through the lens of materialism—and instead to see life as a time for obeying the Lord, serving other people, and preparing ourselves for heaven. When we think like that, it really doesn't make much difference whether we have a lot of money or only a little.

CONCLUSION

SO WHAT?

So what? I have argued that, generally speaking, Christians tend to do well in life, to prosper financially; that when they don't, there's a reason to explain that fact; and that it doesn't matter much to them whether or not they make a lot of money. But one could still ask whether, even if all these things are true, what difference does it make to me? That's a good question. The consequences of any assertion or any doctrine should be considered. Are there any practical consequences of accepting these propositions as true? The points I have made are significant in at least five ways.

An Explanation for Observed Facts

First, what I have written provides an explanation for certain facts. This book is the product of my curiosity. I observed that many Christians have done very well for themselves materially, and I wondered why. Having thought about the reasons for their prosperity, I wondered why others had not done so well. That led me to consider what the Christian's attitude should be towards prospering in this life. My study led me to write what you have read.

People may question some of my assertions, but I don't think they can successfully deny the major thesis of this work—namely, that Christians who make a diligent effort to follow Christ's teachings in the New Testament are more likely to prosper (under ordinary circumstances) than they would if they did not obey those requirements. I believe that this fact provides an explanation for the prosperity that Christians usually enjoy in our society.

A Reason for Gratitude

Second, what has been said gives Christians a reason for gratitude. What should be the response from Christians when they understand that Christ has set them on a way that not only leads to eternal rewards, but also gives them the opportunity to lead the best life possible on this earth—the "abundant life"?

As I have already said, our reaction to our blessings should **not** be pride, but gratitude. If we prosper—if we succeed—in this life, we have nothing to boast of, nothing to be proud about, because we owe everything we are and have to others, and ultimately to God.

- Did we succeed because of our talents or intelligence? If so, where did we get the talents and/or intelligence? Through our genes, from our parents, and ultimately from God, who determined the circumstances of our birth.
- Did we succeed because of our hard work? Who taught us to work hard? Parents? A teacher? A coach? Ultimately God put us under the influence of our mentors.
- Did we overcome great difficulties to succeed? Who

inspired us to do so? A parent? An author? God gave us the opportunity to be inspired.

- Did we get rich because we took advantage of opportunities that came our way? Who gave us the ability to see the potential in those opportunities and the talent to take advantage of them? Who sent the opportunities our direction? God is the answer to both questions.

If we think about it, we must acknowledge the truth that James penned: "Every good gift and every perfect gift is from above, and comes down from the Father of lights, with whom there is no variation or shadow of turning" (Jam 1:17). We must confess that we are unworthy to be so blessed. That attitude will lead us to be grateful to God for all that He has given us and done for us and through us.

Think about it. Isn't it great—and isn't it a great reason to be grateful—that God has given us, through Christ, a great way to live on earth? A way that blesses us with forgiveness and peace, a way that blesses others through us, a way that leads to life eternal, a way that makes available to us the abundant life, and a way that often enables us to prosper materially? Let us thank God for providing for us that way.

A Reminder of Our Responsibilities

Third, what I have written should remind us as Christians of our responsibilities. Christians ought to work hard and Christians ought to be content. In doing so, Christians should aspire to obey the biblical requirements that apply to them. They ought to obey those rules. Hopefully, most Christians do so most of the time. However, being human, we all fail at times. We sin. When we do, we can be grateful that God by His grace, through Christ and His blood, forgives us (1 John 1:7, 9; 2:1, 2).

Nevertheless, as we have previously suggested, our failures as Christians to live up to our high calling may cost us the advantage of being faithful disciples. If, for instance, we are doing well in business, but we are tempted to take an illegal shortcut that will make us more money, and we give in to that temptation, and we are caught, we forfeit benefits that come with living the Christian life. Consequently, at that point in our business career, we will not prosper. Therefore, Christians can use this book to remind them of how they ought to live, of what God expects of them, of what it means to be a Christian. And maybe we can all be encouraged to do the things that are really difficult—to resist the materialistic influences of our age, to be content in all circumstances, to put God's kingdom first in all things, to make the Bible's priorities our priorities, etc.

Another Reason to Share Our Faith

Fourth, what I have pointed out in these pages—namely, the fact that Christianity provides abundant blessings in this life—gives Christians another reason to share their faith with their neighbors. We should be concerned that our friends and families are lost because of the spiritual consequences of being apart from Christ (see, for instance, Eph 2:12). The desire to see them saved so that they can enjoy the hope of heaven should motivate us to seek to share our faith with them.

However, when we are fully convinced that everyone would be better off even in this world if they were Christians, we will (or should be) even more eager to share our faith with others. As a Christian you enjoy the good life, the abundant life. Don't you want your neighbors to enjoy it, too?

An Invitation to Unbelievers

Fifth, I hope that this book will serve as an invitation to non-Christians. Come, become a child of God so that you can enjoy the blessings of the abundant life. Of course, the unbeliever needs to understand that the main reason why he or she needs to accept Christ is that sin has separated us from God, with the result that one is dead in sin (Eph 2:1, 12; Rom 6:23). To be forgiven, one needs to come to Christ through faith (John 8:24) and obedience (Acts 2:38).

Above all, every human being needs to be most concerned about the salvation of his or her soul. However, it's also good to know that the Lord who wants to save you from sin and wants you to live with Him forever, also desires for you to live the best life possible here on this earth. God's requirements are given for the good of humanity. We need to appreciate that fact. We need to understand that what God tells us not to do is not good for us, nor will it bring happiness or success. We also need to understand that what God tells us to do is good for us and will bring us happiness and success.

So I conclude with this invitation to those who have not turned to Jesus. Christ's way has much to offer. Besides giving you salvation, it provides for you an opportunity to lead the happiest, most productive life possible.

SCRIPTURE INDEX

Genesis		2 Samuel		139:7–10	100
2:15	11	4:4	xi(n)		
3:4	51(n)	12:10	93	**Proverbs**	
3:5	51(n)			1:7	46, 52
3:17–19	11	**1 Kings**		2:6	46
12:16	x	21:11–14	xi(n)	2:7	46
13:2	x			3:5–7	46
24:35	x	**2 Kings**		3:5	86
26:13	x	18:19–35	51(n)	3:9	86
30:43	x			3:10	86
45:5	101	**Job**		4:5–9	46
50:20	101	1:21	102	10:4	11
				10:6	46
Exodus		**Psalms**		11:24–26	46
4:11	100	1	xii(n)	12:1	46
19	xi	1:1–3	86	12:15	46
20:17	128	19:10	59	12:27	12
		37:16	xi	13:4	12
		37:17	xi	14:3	46
Leviticus		73	86	14:12	135
12:6–8	xiv	73:3	86	14:23	12
26	xi	73:3–14	xi	15:19	12
26:4	86	119	59	15:22	46
		121:1	65	16:8	xi
Numbers		121:2	65	16:16	46
32:23b	93	128	xii(n)	17:10	46

17:28	46	5:3	34	22:15–22	24
18:9	12	5:5	34	22:17–21	138
19:15	12	5:7–9	34	22:21	24
20:4	12	5:10	xxvi, 141	22:39	35
20:7	46	5:10–12	xvi, 57	23:37–39	121
21:25	12	5:14	25	24:45	47(n)
23:9	46	5:16	37	25	74
24:30–32	12	5:44	60	25:1–13	48
24:33	12	6:10	xvii, 105	25:2	47(n)
24:34	12	6:19	110	25:4	47(n)
26:10	46	6:19–21	xv, 134	25:8	47(n)
28:19	12	6:20	61, 110	25:9	47(n)
29:11	46	6:21	79(n)	25:14–30	69
		6:25	59, 123	25:24	70
Ecclesiastes		6:33	xix, 59, 123, 140	25:25	70
2:11	133			25:31–46	78
12:13	133	7:7–9	xvii, 124	26:39	xvii
		7:7–11	65	26:41b	94
Isaiah		7:12a	35	26:42	xvii
53:5	xiii(n)	7:13	34	27:57–60	xiv
		7:13–14	43	28:20	57, 123
Jeremiah		7:14	54		
12:1	xi	7:24	48	**Mark**	
		9:29	xxi	3:5	121
Ezekiel		10:16	47, 47(n)	3:31–35	136
18:32	101(n)	10:16–23	xvi	4:1	xiv
33:11	101(n)	13:1, 2	xiv	4:19	xv
		14:27	60	6:2	48
Habakkuk		16:24	56–57, 139	6:3	xiv
1:4	xi	16:26	127	6:50	60
1:13	xi	17:24–27	24(n)	10:28	xxiii(n)
1:13b	86	19:22	127	10:29–30	xxii
		19:23	127	12:30	80
Matthew		19:24	xv	16:15–16	xxvi

Scripture Index

16:20	xiii	10:10	xxi	8	50
		11:35	121	8:1–3	xvi
Luke		13:12–17	139	8:22	30
1:53	xv	13:34	57, 61, 137	9:36	57
2:7	xiv	13:35	34, 57, 137	9:37	57
2:24	xiv	14:15	37	10	50
3:14	119	14:27b	59–60	11:28–30	58
4:16–21	xv	15:17	57	12	xvi
6:20	xv	15:18–20	xvi	12:12	65, 117
6:35	xviii	17:16	133	13	50
6:38	xxiii, xxiv	18:33–38	138	16:20	25
8:1–3	xiv	18:36	25	16:21	25
8:14	140	19:12	24	16:25	124
10:20	139	19:23–24	xiv	17	50
12:13–15	128	20:30–31	xiii	17:4	117
12:15	127			17:6–7	25
12:15–21	xv	**Acts**		17:16	121
12:16–19	128–129	2	50, 78	17:27	100
12:20	129	2–5	116	17:28	100
12:21	129, 134	2:38	xxvi, 57, 63, 147	18:13	25
12:42	47(n)			19:23–40	25
14:26	136	2:44	58	20:32	59
15	93	2:45	58	20:33–35	126(n)
16:8	47, 47(n)	2:47	136	20:35	79
16:14	xv	3	xiv(n)	21:14	103
16:19–31	xv	4	xvi, 78	21:38	25
19:10	xii	4:23–31	65	24:5	25
23:34	60	4:32–37	58	25:8	25
		5	xvi, 78		
John		5:4	76	**Romans**	
1:46	xiv	5:28	27	1:10	103
3:16	xii, 61	5:29	27, 138	1:16	xix
6:60b	97	5:32	57	3:23	63(n), 93
8:24	147	7	xvi, 51(n)	6:23	147

8:28	xxii, 53, 62, 63, 100, 105, 123, 140	10:13	xxii, 103, 123	6:10	78
8:31	62	10:15	47(n)	**Ephesians**	
8:35	62	12	72	1:17	48
8:37–39	62	12:13	136	2:1	147
10:1	121	13:4	34	2:12	146, 147
12	72	13:5a	34	2:15	xi
12:1	80	15:26	64	3:16	57, 134
12:2a	133	16:1	78, 116	3:17	57
12:3–7	33	16:2	78, 116	4	34
12:5	58	16:9	74(n)	4:6	100
12:10	58	**2 Corinthians**		4:25–32	34–35
12:15	106	4:16	134	4:28	11(n), 77, 115, 116
12:18	25	8	xxiv, 58	5:1	37
12:19–21	60	8:2	78	5:15	48
13:1	138	8:9	xxiv	5:16	48, 74
13:1–7	25–26	9	xxiv, 58	5:25	136
14:19	58	9:7	78	6:5–8	13
15:4	45	9:8–11	78	6:9	16
15:25–27	58	11:23–26	xvi		
15:32	103	12:7–9	xiv	**Philippians**	
16:23	117	**Galatians**		1:21	64
1 Corinthians		1:8–9	xix	1:23	64, 134
1:18	54	1:10	135	2:5	139
1:18–25	45	2:20	80, 137	2:5–8	xxiv
1:26	117	3:14	x	2:6–8	139
2	45	3:23–25	45	3:4b	137
3:10	48–49	3:24–25	xi	3:7	137
4:19	103	4:6	57	3:8	137
6:19	71, 80	5:19–26	137	3:13	80, 121
6:20	71, 80	5:22	60	3:14	80, 121
9:19–22	49	5:22–23a	34	4:3	139
10:11	45	6:2	57	4:4	67, 122

Scripture Index

4:6	59	3:12	57	2:3–4	xiii
4:7	60, 122	3:15	136	3:13	58
4:11	89	5:8	115	10:24	58
4:11b–13	120	5:23	xiv	10:25	58, 65
4:13	61	6:1–2	14	11:13	113
		6:5	126(n)	11:14	135

Colossians

		6:6–8	120	11:16	135
1:11	60	6:6–10	125–126	11:25	134, 140
1:13	138	6:8	89	11:26	134, 140
1:27	57	6:9	xviii, 130	12:1–2	44
3:1b	133	6:10	xvii, xxvi, 130	13:5	57, 120, 123
3:2	133	6:15	138		
3:5	127	6:17	130	**James**	
3:12–14	35	6:17–19	117, 129–130	1:5	48, 53, 124
3:16	58			1:13	103(n)
3:22–25	13			1:13–15	139
4:1	16	**2 Timothy**		1:14	103(n)
4:6	48	3:12	xvii, xxvi	1:15	103(n)
		3:16	45	1:17	8, 145
1 Thessalonians		3:17	45	1:19b	46(n)
2:4	135	4:3	xix	1:27	78, 133
5:11	58	4:7	123, 139	3:14–16	45
5:14	58	4:8	123, 139	3:17	48, 53
5:16	122	4:20	xiv	3:18	48, 53
5:17	105, 122			4:2b	65
5:18	122	**Titus**		4:3	xvii
		1:10	126(n)	4:13–15	103–104
2 Thessalonians		1:11	126(n)	5:13	124
1:4–6	xvi			5:16	58
3:10	11, 115–116	**Hebrews**			
		1:1–2	xi	**1 Peter**	
1 Timothy		1:2	100	1:18	80
1:15	xii	1:3	100	1:19	80
2:1–3	26–27	1:14	57	2:9	136

[153]

2:11	133	2:15a	133
2:13–17	26	4:7	57
2:17	138	4:18	60
2:18	13	5:14	65, 124
2:21	37, 139		
2:24	xiii(n)	**3 John**	
3:17	103	2	xx
4:9	58		
4:10	58, 72	**Revelation**	
4:11	72	2	139
4:12–14	xvi	2:10	61, 82, 139, 140
4:15	xvi		
4:19	xvi, 103	2:28	139
5:7	60	3	139
		3:21	139
2 Peter		7:14	xvi
1:4	59	13:8	139
1:5–7	35, 137	20:12	139
1:10	114	20:15	139
2:3	126(n)	21:4	64, 135
2:14	126(n)	21:8	37, 128
3:9	101(n)	21:27	139
3:18	137		

1 John

1:7	44, 63, 146
1:7–9	82
1:8	30, 94
1:8–10	43
1:9	146
1:10	30
2:1	146
2:2	146

www.ingramcontent.com/pod-product-compliance
Lightning Source LLC
Chambersburg PA
CBHW030324080526
44584CB00012B/691